PRAISE FOR "POP GOES R[]

"Terry Mattingly is arguably this country's most judicious commentator on the interface between religion and popular culture; and in *Pop Goes Religion*, he gives us the best of his best. In equal parts entertaining and informative, these pieces and Mattingly's running commentary about the context of each celebrate America's deep, if sometimes idiosyncratic, absorption with all things religious."

PHYLLIS TICKLE
Religion Editor (ret.), *Publishers Weekly* and compiler of *The Divine Hours*

"As this excellent collection of essays demonstrates, Terry Mattingly understands that finding faith in popular culture is no trivial pursuit. These columns remain fresh and relevant. They were so informative, I found myself taking notes!"

MARK I. PINSKY
Author of *The Gospel According to Disney*

"Terry Mattingly's astonishingly broad grasp of popular culture is matched by an impressive talent for writing with fairness and insight, even about things that would have most of us tearing our hair out. Get on board for a wild ride with the best of guides."

FREDERICA MATHEWES-GREEN
Beliefnet.com columnist and National Review Online movie critic

"This is a book I've been waiting for. A must-read for anyone who hopes to communicate faith to a society mesmerized by pop culture, and for anyone else who wants to plumb the depths of the stuff on their MP3 players and TiVos and at their local multiplex. Terry Mattingly is a uniquely acute observer of both pop culture and religion who *inhabits* both worlds simultaneously, spotting the parallels, conflicts, and convergences. He is the theologian invading 'Entertainment Tonight,' the pop culture fan who understands and reveals the world of church, synagogue, and mosque."

BISHOP WILLIAM C. FREY
Author of *The Dance of Hope*

He gets it. Terry Mattingly—of GetReligion.org, among many other good works—gets the spirit and flavor and texture of those improbable locations where religion and modern culture encounter and circle each other: not quite enemies, not quite friends. In "Pop Goes Religion," he makes very certain you get it, too.

WILLIAM MURCHISON
Radford Distinguished Professor of Journalism, Baylor University

If there's a Christian writing today who understands better than Terry Mattingly the complex relationship between religion and popular culture, I don't know who he is. Mattingly has a veteran journalist's unerring eye for discerning the deeper issues and forces at work among believers today, and writes with a missionary urgency about the challenges and crises that arise when pulpit meets public square.

—ROD DREHER,
Dallas Morning News columnist and author of "Crunchy Cons"

Terry Mattingly is probably the only religion writer in America who's as much at home in floor seats at a U2 show as he is on the floor of the annual convocation for any given denomination. He clearly has an affinity for pop culture, and no one makes a better case for the church needing to become more aware of the media its congregants are consuming. But Mattingly also possesses a healthy skepticism about the mingling of faith and entertainment, and he isn't one of those guys who's naive enough to imagine the problems of the church being solved by more sermons about movies. If anyone is equipped to keep an eye on this balancing act of spirituality and culture, it's somebody who knows every theological distinction you could think of AND all the lyrics to "Bullet the Blue Sky."

—CHRIS WILLMAN,
senior writer, Entertainment Weekly, and author of
"Rednecks & Bluenecks: The Politics of Country Music"

"I recommend this book to everyone who wants to know about the exciting way in which Christian faith is interacting with the world of popular entertainment and culture."

PHILLIP JOHNSON
Author of *Reason in the Balance* and *Darwin on Trial*

POP ★ GOES
RELIGION

POP ★ GOES RELIGION

FAITH IN POPULAR CULTURE
★ TERRY MATTINGLY ★

GENERAL EDITOR: MARK JOSEPH

W PUBLISHING GROUP
A Division of Thomas Nelson Publishers
Since 1798

www.wpublishinggroup.com

Published by W Publishing Group, a division of Thomas Nelson, Inc., P.O. Box 141000, Nashville, TN 37214.

W Publishing Group books may be purchased in bulk for educational, business, fund-raising, or sales promotional use. For information, please e-mail SpecialMarkets@ThomasNelson.com.

Editorial Staff: Jennifer Stair; Bethany Bothman
Cover Design: David Carlson, Gearbox Design, Sisters, OR
Published in association with Bully Pulpit Books.

All articles are reprinted with permission of Scripps Howard News Service.

Scripture quotations in this book are taken from The Holy Bible, New International Version®. Copyright © 1973, 1978, 1984 by International Bible Society. Used by permission of Zondervan. All rights reserved.

Library of Congress Cataloging-in-Publication Data

Mattingly, Terry.
    Pop goes religion / by Terry Mattingly.
       p. cm.
    Includes index.
    ISBN 0-8499-0998-8
    1. Religion and culture—United States. 2. Popular culture—United
States. I. Title.
BL65.C8M365 2005
201'.7'0973—dc22

2005006487

Printed in the United States of America

05 06 07 08 09 RRD 9 8 7 6 5 4 3 2 1

With gratitude to Roberta Green,
a good reporter

CONTENTS

EDITOR'S NOTE

Terry Mattingly is a journalist's journalist. If you want to find out what he believes by reading his columns, good luck. He's always balanced and fair, and he leaves out his opinion in favor of the person he's interviewing. I first met Terry a decade ago when I was being interviewed for one of his columns and noticed this quality about him right away. Terry believes that God and religion are important, but he also sees the value of pop culture and the need for people of faith to understand and be present in pop culture. Anytime religion and pop culture converge, he is there with pen and notebook ready to chronicle what he sees for the rest of us.

I really couldn't think of a more fitting book to launch the "Bully Pulpit" book series than Terry's "Pop Goes Religion." I have been prodding Terry to write this book for at least eight years and am honored to be able to play a role in its release.

"Bully pulpit" was a term coined by one of my heroes, Teddy Roosevelt, who used the term "bully" to mean good and "pulpit" to mean a place from which to give one's opinions. Declaring the presidency to be a "bully pulpit," Roosevelt used his high office to argue passionately for his convictions. In much the same way, this series will allow passionate writers who specialize in topics where pop culture and faith intersect to bring important ideas to our collective attention.

Special thanks to Kate Etue for editorial patience, Michael Ramirez for an outstanding logo and Rob Stennett for skilled editing.

MARK JOSEPH
General Editor,
"Bully Pulpit" book series

FOREWORD

As a Hollywood producer I am often asked how I am able to reconcile my love for God with a job that frequently has me working with people who often disagree with my beliefs. To me the answer is simple: God has given me an ability to produce movies and television, and I want to do it for his glory.

Sometimes my movies reflect my faith in God; other times I'm just telling a great story. In both cases, I'm doing what God created me to do.

Terry Mattingly's "Pop Goes Religion" is a look into the lives of people like me who have decided to take their gifts and put them to work in the center of the popular media culture. Some may be concerned that this will result in the trivialization of God, Jesus, faith and all that is sacred. Others disagree — believing that when Jesus' Great Commission is to be taken literally, the message is to be taken everywhere including cartoons, comic books, rock music, movies, books, television, the Internet and any other means of communication available to us today. Read the book and decide for yourself.

Reading Terry's book, I am intrigued by J.R.R. Tolkien and his passion for the written word, grateful that C.S. Lewis brought his faith to bear on the Narnia Chronicles, amazed at the fortitude it took for Mel Gibson to bring "The Passion" to the big screen, and surprised to learn that Van Halen was once fronted by a singer who was as passionate in his love for God as he was for rock music.

From VeggieTales to "The Simpsons," Harry Potter to "The Matrix," Terry Mattingly chronicles just how common it has become to find God in popular culture. Like a prophet of old, Terry Mattingly is telling us the story of how God has refused to cooperate with those who think he shouldn't be a part of popular entertainment.

Join me at this intersection of faith and culture, and watch how Terry gets it right, asking the questions that make this place uncertain and affirming at the same time.

RALPH WINTER
Producer,
"X-Men" movies,
"Fantastic Four"

INTRODUCTION

Jesus just left Chicago and he's bound for New Orleans.
Well now, Jesus just left Chicago and he's bound for New Orleans.
Workin' from one end to the other and all points in between.
— ZZ TOP[1]

Pick up any modern newspaper, and you can read what is happening in the world of entertainment. Pick up the nation's best newspapers, and you can read about the latest news in the world of religion, both in the United States and abroad.

But what happens if you try to put these two worlds together? I happen to think that some of the most interesting stories on the entertainment beat today have to do with religion. At the same time, some of the most interesting stories on what professionals often call the Godbeat have to do with what is going on in what many people still think is the Godforsaken world of entertainment.

So there you have it. That sort of explains why this book exists.

However, to really get in sync with what follows in these pages, you need to picture in your mind's eye the following bizarre scene from my life as a journalist. This will be complicated, so hang on.

It is the summer of 1986, and I am camped out near the elevators of a fine hotel in downtown Denver, waiting for the city's first glimpse of Bishop J. Francis Stafford of Memphis, Tenn., who has just been named as the new archbishop of Denver. Stafford is a complex and interesting man, a first-round draft pick of the Catholic ecclesiastical and intellectual establishment in his hometown of Baltimore. After a decade in Denver, he became a cardinal and moved to one of the top slots in the Vatican.

However, when it comes to popular culture, Stafford would be the first to confess that he has no credibility — zero, zip, nada — on the street or at the mall.

Once, while driving to work, he found himself behind a car with a bumper sticker that read: "John Lennon Lives!" The archbishop was curious about the meaning of this phrase, and as he later told the story, he turned into Denver's famous Tattered Cover Book Store to do some research. You see, he did not know who John Lennon was, and he also had no idea why some people needed to have faith that he was still alive, as a person or as a metaphor. I never had the courage to ask him if he had heard of the Beatles.

Stafford is not alone. I have met quite a few powerful shepherds who know little or nothing about the media forces that dominate the lives of the people in their flocks. Hold on to that idea for a few pages.

So I am waiting outside that elevator for a simple, journalistic reason. This Stafford fellow is about to become the biggest religious figure in Denver — a very competitive news town — and I want to be the journalist who gets the first interview.

The rest of the media is waiting in the lobby and outside the building. However, a source inside the archdiocese staff has told me when Stafford plans to leave the hotel, and with that information, it was easy to figure out which elevator he would almost certainly be using. So I'm thinking that, if I play my cards right, when the elevator doors open, I may be able to quietly steer this future prince of the church around the corner into a conference room and get that interview. Then I might even be able to kindly point him toward a side door out of the hotel, helping him avoid the rest of the media horde and, by the way, making my interview an exclusive. Reporters do things like that.

There I am, poised, watching the elevator doors with serious intent.

All of a sudden, my stalking-the-headline reverie is broken by a somewhat familiar-sounding voice behind me, speaking with a deep-fried Texas drawl. The voice asks this strange question: "Port Arthur Teen Club, right?"

Lo and behold, there stood a sharply dressed man whose face and beard would be familiar to anyone who watched MTV in the 1980s or who has paid any attention whatsoever to classic music videos. He is pointing at me.

It is Billy J. Gibbons, the lead singer-guitarist for the bluesy trio called ZZ Top, which has since been enshrined in the Rock and Roll Hall of Fame. ZZ Top is in town playing a show, so Gibbons has just returned from a sound check at the nearby arena. He's wearing an ultraloud red satin ZZ Top roadie tour jacket, a ZZ Top baseball hat, and some not-so-cheap ZZ Top sunglasses. His trademark waist-length beard is, of course, combed out really fine. This man stands out in a crowd.

Now, the reason I know Gibbons is that I grew up as a Southern Baptist preacher's kid in the Texas Gulf Coast refinery town of Port Arthur.

I guess that takes some explaining, too.

You see, Southern Baptists back then didn't dance, and for all I know, that may still be true of Southern Baptist preachers' kids — unless they dance to the Christian rock bands that play in the main church services these days. (Isn't that ironic?) But back when I was in high school in the early 1970s, the deacons' kids would turn a "PK" over to the Baptist powers that be really quick if you so much as shimmied in a public place.

So I knew nothing at all about dancing. But I still went to the hot local music joint — that would be the Port Arthur Teen Club — to pay close attention to what was happening onstage. In other words, I actually listened to the music. Plus, some of my friends had a band that was good enough to be the warm-up act for the top bands in the region. I used to help them set up their equipment before the shows and then hang around to help the main band on the marquee.

This is how I met the guys in the hottest band on the Gulf Coast during those years — ZZ Top.

A decade later, I used that Port Arthur Teen Club connection to work my way past the security personnel for an interview with Gibbons and company when they played at Assembly Hall at the University of Illinois at Urbana-Champaign. That was while I was writing a weekly column on rock music for the local daily newspaper. One of the most interesting groups I got to interview during those years was an intense, seriously postpunk quartet of Irish guys in a panel truck. The young U2 was bouncing around the country playing small halls in support of their new album, called "October," which was about all kinds of things, like God, death, heaven, hell and the terrors of adolescence. But that's another story.

Anyway, the point is that I was a music fanatic who enjoyed writing a rock column for several years before I started covering the religion-news beat full time in Charlotte, N.C., and then in Denver.

So that's why Gibbons recognized me that day at the hotel elevators in Denver. He knew I was a journalist. But I was also a journalist who, as a kid, used to lug around his guitars and amplifiers at the Port Arthur Teen Club.

Gibbons barely had time to say, "What in the world are you doing out here?" when, sure enough, the elevator doors opened and out walked the new archbishop. Since Gibbons and I were standing in the way, Stafford stopped and looked us over. At the same time, Gibbons checked out the archbishop's threads. Roman Catholic prelates stand out in a crowd, too.

Try hard to picture that scene. These two men are high priests in radically different churches.

After a few awkward seconds, I did the first thing that came into my mind. I introduced myself to the archbishop, asked if he had a few moments he could spare for an interview — he said yes — and then turned and did the next round of introductions.

"Uh, Bishop Stafford, this is Billy Gibbons of ZZ Top. Perhaps you've seen them on MTV. Uh, Mr. Gibbons, this is Bishop J. Francis Stafford, the new archbishop of Denver. He's moving here from Memphis."

As it turned out, Gibbons knew Memphis quite well, but not for the same reasons as the archbishop. After all, there may be more blues guitarists in the city of Memphis than there are Roman Catholics. That may even be in the census data.

We chatted for a minute, and then Gibbons said something that perfectly summed up that moment for me. You can consider this the "mission statement" for this book, if you wish.

"Wait a minute," said Gibbons. "You went from interviewing people like me to interviewing people like him?"

Yes, I did, I said. It was an interesting career move.

But, you see, I never stopped being interested in what rock stars and other entertainers had to say about issues of life and death, joy and sorrow, heaven and hell. I also became more and more interested in what all of those archbishops and other mainstream religious leaders said — or didn't say — about the world of entertainment and popular culture.

These were, you see, the two halves of my journalistic life.

Bishop Stafford, meet Billy Gibbons. Of course, I realize that you have probably never heard of each other.

Please understand that there are so many other introductions I wish I could make. Most of the people who run our newsrooms and studios struggle to understand the role that faith plays in this culture. Then again, the overwhelming majority of the leaders of mainstream religion have a love-hate relationship with mass media.

So Peter Jackson, say hello to the Catholic traditionalist J.R.R. Tolkien. Carl Sagan, meet Billy Graham. Robert Duvall, meet Bob Briner. Rene Russo, meet Mother Teresa. The list goes on and on.

So I kept writing about music and entertainment, even after I switched over to covering the religion beat. I have always been fascinated with the tensions between these two crucial parts of American life — the world of organized religion and the world of mass media. And there is more to this than the important issue of what happens or fails to happen when mainstream news professionals try to cover stories of faith.

As a journalist, I care about the news. But I can also read statistics about the stark realities of American life, and, like it or not, the statistics all point toward the power of the entertainment media that shape our popular culture. That threatens journalists, but it also scares preachers.

That's why I used to tell my news editors that we needed to do a better job covering what happens when popular authors begin writing books about angels and Oprah starts lighting candles and waving her hands in the air while she prays to the universe. Journalists everywhere have written lots of novelty stories about George Lucas, "Star Wars" and the Force. Nevertheless, I think that few truly recognize that moviegoers are wrestling with religious issues week after week when, to paraphrase the great American film director Frank Capra, they sit listening to sermons in dark theaters.

Back in the 1980s, the mainstream media paid close attention to the rise and fall of the televangelists, but editors didn't seem to realize that the scandals were fueled by the rising influence of television and popular culture in the lives of ordinary evangelical Christians — even the elderly. Then all those new Protestant "megachurches" started hiring drummers and hanging up giant screens to show clips of movies like "The Matrix." That's a mass-media story, too. In the 1990s, we entered an age in which some conservative Christian groups actually changed the schedules of their Bible studies so that the faithful didn't have to miss a night of "ER" or "Friends."

People are worshipping at all kinds of new altars. Journalists and preachers cannot afford to ignore that.

The bottom line: If you study the statistics, the typical modern American is much more likely to be exposed to a new religious insight or doctrine at the mall or the movie multiplex than in a traditional sanctuary. This is how modern Americans spend their time, spend their money and make their decisions. Day by day, they have evolved into mass-media disciples.

I'm not the only person who thinks that. Here's what the oft-quoted evangelical pollster George Barna, writing with e-commerce specialist Mark Hatch, had to say about this issue in the book "Boiling Point: Monitoring Cultural Shifts in the 21st Century":

> The world of entertainment and mass communications — through television, radio, contemporary music, movies, magazines, art, video games and pop literature — is indisputably the most extensive and influential theological training system in the world. From commercials to sitcoms, from biographies to hit songs, from computer simulation games to talk shows, God's principles are challenged every moment of every day, in very entertaining, palatable and discreet ways. Few Christians currently have the intellectual and spiritual tools to identify and reject the garbage.[2]

The problem is that Hatch and Barna, in the rest of their book, have nothing else to say about this topic. They opened that door and then quietly closed it, with no further comment about the big idea they had just articulated. As journalists would say, they buried their lead. Perhaps the subject was just too frightening.

As a reporter and as a teacher, I have tried to prop open the door between the world of faith and the world of entertainment.

As the 1980s ended, two things happened that led directly to the content of this book. First, I started writing a weekly column called "On Religion" for the national news feature wire of the Scripps

Howard News Service in Washington, D.C. Then, a year or two later, I left the newsroom of the Denver Rocky Mountain News to begin teaching as "communicator on culture" at Denver Seminary. This move was inspired, in large part, by the work of two towering figures in Christian education — the counselor and progressive evangelical thinker Dr. Vernon Grounds and Dr. Haddon Robinson, a communication scholar and author of the famous textbook "Biblical Preaching."

After spending some time trying to explain religion to many of my editors, we decided to try to convince religious leaders to study the mass media. We are still beating our heads on that wall.

But what about my weekly column? I wondered if I could keep writing it. My longtime editor at Scripps Howard, Walter Veazey, graciously urged me to continue doing so, even though I was no longer working in the newsroom.

Within a matter of weeks, I was on the telephone with him with another question: Would it be OK if I increased the number of columns I wrote about the intersection of faith and popular culture? We decided that I would give it a shot, while trying not to ignore more conventional religion-news topics. After all, I am a religion writer, not an entertainment writer.

After a year or two, I decided I would try to average writing one entertainment-media-driven column a month. However, it soon became obvious that it would be hard not to write more than that. Now, well into my second decade writing the column, there are scores of these columns on faith and popular culture.

The thing about news writing is that this craft automatically links one's work to a very specific time, with articles marching through the calendar week after week. Thus, the contents of this book represent a quick overview of what I have written in the past decade, gathered into collections focusing on popular music, movies, television, books and the general influence of popular culture on the church and family. The columns talk about the news of the day, but they also contain the voices of artists, thinkers and entertainers whose views have helped shape our times. The voices are still interesting, and what they have to say still matters.

Please think of this as a collection of snapshots from the front lines of the pop-culture wars. Along the way, I will offer some additional commentary to help you place these articles in context and paint some broader themes.

You cannot write a thousand or so columns without needing to thank plenty of people. I must name a few who have most influenced this book, beginning with the aforementioned Dr. Vernon Grounds, Dr. Haddon Robinson and Walter Veazey. I should also thank my mentor in journalism long ago at Baylor University, Prof. David McHam, and Dr. James W. Carey, who did so much to encourage my work at the University of Illinois. The Scripps Howard "On Religion" column would never have been created without the support of the late Ralph Looney at the Rocky Mountain News and longtime Scripps Howard CEO William Burleigh. I must thank other friends and colleagues who have helped through the years, beginning with Dr. Quentin Schultze at Calvin College and, in recent years, Dr. Joseph Webb at the new School of Communication and Media at Palm Beach Atlantic University. It is impossible to dig into these topics without being influenced by scholars such as Drs. Martin Marty, Stewart Hoover and James Davison Hunter.

I have a special sense of affection and appreciation for Drs. Sue Crider Atkins and Richard Gathro and the rest of the always-patient journalism team at the Council for Christian Colleges and Universities. And then there are my friends at the great online newsroom water cooler, beginning with Frederica Mathewes-Green, Rod Dreher, Douglas LeBlanc, Peggy Noonan, Chris Willman, Mark Joseph and many others. What would we do without e-mail and, these days, weblogs?

But most of all, I must thank my loved ones, near and far, for putting up with a journalist in the family. My father, Bert Mattingly, was a pastor, and my mother is a language-arts teacher. That explains a lot, I think. And there is no way to offer adequate thanks to my librarian wife, Debra, and our children, Sarah Jeanne and Frye Lewis, for understanding why I have not been able to have any fun whatsoever on Tuesdays ("Oh, right, it's column night") for nearly two decades.

Under the Mercy,
tmatt
www.tmatt.net
www.getreligion.org

GOD AND POPULAR MUSIC

One of the most controversial issues inside the religious-media niche can be summed up with this question: What is "Christian music"? I discovered one answer in a highly unlikely place during the 2002 academic year — the weight room at the Christian college at which I was teaching at the time.

In order to have some aging baby boomer music for the gym sound system, I started bringing discs full of up-tempo "Christian songs" by artists like Bob Dylan, Bruce Cockburn, T-Bone Burnett, Mark Heard and Wynonna Judd. One of these mixes offered 80 minutes of highly religious material by U2.

After a month or two, I was told, in no uncertain terms, that this was not acceptable. Only "Christian music" could be used. At that point, the mass-media professor side of me started asking the gym personnel to define their terms.

The big problem, they said, was the U2 disc (although my others flunked, too). U2 was not a "Christian band." I said that I was well aware of that. U2 is a band in which the songs are written by Christians. That didn't matter, I was told.

Days later, I heard the following lyrics crash out on the weight-room sound system:

> *In the locust wind comes a rattle and hum*
> *Jacob wrestled the angel and the angel was overcome*
> *You plant a demon seed*
> *You raise a flower of fire*
> *You see them burning crosses*
> *You see the flames higher and higher.*[1]

Wait a minute, I said. That's a U2 song called "Bullet the Blue Sky."

Right, said the manager. But U2 wasn't performing the song. This version was by P.O.D., and at that moment in time, this band's music was being sold in Christian bookstores. The notes and the words were the same, but now the song was acceptable.

I gave up.

There is another way to answer this question. The Gospel Music Association started a ruckus when it defined gospel music as "music in any style whose lyric is substantially based on historically orthodox Christian truth contained in or derived from the Holy Bible; and/or an expression of worship of God or praise for his works; and/or testimony of relationship with God through Christ; and/or obviously prompted and informed by a Christian world view."[2]

That's nice, but that isn't the definition the authorities were using in that weight room, or it would have been acceptable to listen to U2 or to Johnny Cash sing gospel. For that matter, there was even a time when the rock band Van Halen had a born-again singer named Gary Cherone belting out lyrics rooted in the third chapter of the Epistle of James. If you talk to the man, he's very upfront about what he was doing.

"I knew exactly what the words meant and where they were coming from," said Cherone, who is also known to MTV fans for his work with the band Extreme. "I mean, just read the words — it's all there. Thou shalt not commit false witness. It's a song about lying and gossiping. The words had to work in a rock song, but I certainly wasn't trying to hide anything."

Cherone started quoting a snippet of the lyrics that swirl through the mix at the end of a rocker called "Fire in the Hole." Here they are:

> *Rudder of ship, which sets the course.*
> *Does not the bit, bridle the horse?*
> *Great is the forest, set by a small flame.*
> *Like a tongue on fire, no one can tame.*[3]

It doesn't take a degree in New Testament studies to figure that out. It would seem that an obvious Bible quote such as this would fit within the GMA definition of "gospel music." So why didn't Van Halen get a Dove? The album liner notes even included a nod to super-Calvinist theologian R.C. Sproul.

Cherone laughed out loud. Van Halen fans, he noted, would have been just as scandalized by a Dove nod as the GMA committee members. It would have been fun.

"I thought that the 'bit to the horse' part of the lyric was especially obvious," said Cherone. "But when you stop and think about it, what's the big deal? Dylan's been weaving Bible verses into his songs for several decades now. There's nothing new about this.

Truth is, there are at least six or seven competing definitions of "Christian music" being used these days in a marketplace ruled by preachers and lawyers. I dare you, in this part of the book, to try to figure out who is using what definition:

1. "Christian music" consists of hymns.
2. If music can be played or sung in worship services, then it's "Christian."

3. "Christian music" can be found in all genres of music, except rock. Anything with a strong backbeat is off-limits.

4. All forms of music are acceptable, even heavy-metal rock or rap, as long as the songs contain clear evangelistic messages.

5. "Christian songs" must contain some clear "God-talk." Many Contemporary Christian Music industry pros call this the "Jesus per minute" rule.

6. "Christian music" is music made by artists who are publicly identified as believers, and their art — to one degree or another — reflects this Christian worldview.

U2 frontman Bono has another definition. He once told me that he thinks "Christian music" doesn't exist. Why? It's arrogant for sinful people — he put himself at the top of that list — to sell their music by using the label "Christian" as a marketing device.

Good luck figuring it all out.

Then you'll be ready to talk about "Christian movies" and "Christian television."

U2 BEDEVILS THE MODERN CHURCH

January 2002

It happened at the moment in U2's "Zoo TV" show where Bono did his "Elvis-devil dance," decked out in a glittering gold Las Vegas lounge suit and tacky red horns.

As usual, the charismatic singer pulled some girl out of the crowd to cavort with Mister MacPhisto, this devilish alter ego. On this night in Wales, his dance partner had her own agenda, Bono told the Irish Times.

"Are you still a believer?" she asked. "If so, what are you doing dressed up as the devil?"

Bono gave her a serious answer as the music roared on. "Have you read 'The Screwtape Letters,' a book by C.S. Lewis that a lot of intense Christians are plugged into? They are letters from the devil. That's where I got the whole philosophy of 'mock-the-devil-and-he-will-flee-from-you,'" replied Bono, referring to U2's ironic, video-drenched tours in the 1990s.

Yes, the girl said, she had read "The Screwtape Letters." She understood that Lewis had turned sin inside out in order to make a case for faith.

"Then you know what I am doing," said Bono.

It's highly unlikely Mister MacPhisto will make an appearance when U2 rocks the Super Bowl XXXVI halftime show. During their "Elevation" tour, U2 performed on a stage shaped like a heart, and Bono opened the shows by kneeling in prayer. He began the anthem "Where the Streets Have No Name" by quoting from Psalm 116, and shows ended with shouts of "Praise! Unto the Almighty!"

But whatever happens in New Orleans, U2's presence almost guarantees that people will dissect it in church coffee hours as well as at water coolers. Plenty of believers remain convinced Bono's devil suit was more than symbolic.

"I think they have been clear — for nearly 25 years now — about the role that Christian faith plays in their music. They're not hiding anything," said the Rev. Steve Stockman, the Presbyterian chaplain at Queen's University in Belfast, Northern Ireland. He is the author of "Walk On: The Spiritual Journey of U2" and hosts BBC's "Rhythm and Soul" radio program.

"At the same time, they have always left big spiritual questions hanging out there — unanswered. That is an interesting way to talk about art, and that's an interesting way to live out your faith, especially when you're trying to do it in front of millions of people."

Stockman has never met the band. Still, there is no shortage of source material since Bono, in particular, has never been able to keep his mouth shut when it comes to sin, grace, temptation, damnation, salvation, revelation or the general state of the universe. Two others — drummer Larry Mullen Jr. and guitarist Dave "The Edge" Evans — have long identified themselves as Christians. Bassist Adam Clayton remains a spiritual free agent.

The key, said Stockman, is that U2 emerged in Dublin, Ireland, in a culturally Catholic land in which it was impossible to be sucked into an evangelical subculture of "Christian news," "Christian radio" and "Christian music." The tiny number of Protestants prevented the creation of a "Christian" marketplace.

Thus, U2 plunged into real rock 'n' roll because that was the only game in town. U2 didn't collide with the world of Contemporary Christian Music until its first American tours. Then all hell broke loose.

While the secular press rarely ridicules the band's faith, noted Stockman, the "Christian press and Christians in general have been the doubters" who were keen to "denounce the band's Christian members as lost." Many have heaped "condemnation on their lifestyles, which include smoking cigars, drinking Jack Daniels and using language that is not common currency at Southern Baptist conventions."

It's crucial that most U2 controversies center on lifestyle issues. But Stockman is convinced that deeper divisions center on what Bono and company are saying — in word and deed — about the church's retreat from art, media and popular culture.

The contemporary church "has put a spiritual hierarchy on jobs," said Stockman. "Ministers and missionaries are on top, then perhaps doctors and nurses come next and so on to the bottom, where artists appear. Artists of whatever kind have to compromise everything to entertain. Art is fluffy froth that is no good in the kingdom of God. What nonsense."

AT THE CROSSROADS — DO THE MATH

January 1999

As she pulled into traffic, Elaine Benes turned on her boyfriend's car radio and began bouncing along to the music.

Then the lyrics sank in: "Jesus is one, Jesus is all. Jesus, pick me up when I fall." In horror, she punched another button, then another. "Jesus," she muttered, discovering they all were set to Christian stations. Then the scene jumped to typical "Seinfeld" restaurant chat.

"I like Christian rock," said the ultracynical George Costanza. "It's very positive. It's not like those real musicians who think they're so cool and hip."

Notice how the lords of Must See TV stuck in the knife and gave it a sneaky little twist, noted rocker Charlie Peacock, who has two decades of experience in both the secular and sacred markets. Contemporary Christian Music — or CCM — is "positive," not "cool" or "hip." It's nice, meek and safe. After all, these aren't "real" musicians.

"Positive and nice. Helpful and friendly," writes Peacock, in his book "At the Crossroads," about the identity crisis in the thriving CCM industry. "Sounds more like a description of the Ace Hardware man than music informed by a story so . . . real that it involves every action, emotion and thought under the sun — a complex, bloody, beautiful, redemptive, truthful story."

Since Christendom is built on a story that is literally larger than life, Peacock wonders why CCM is smaller than life. The Bible is full of sin, death, doubt, love, hate, anger, war, lust and other messy subjects. The faith of the ages wrestles with the bad news before reaching the Good News. Yet many Nashville executives would agree with the "Seinfeld" gang that CCM products must be tamer than the "real" pop, country and rock albums they mimic. Truth is, no one expects

CCM to appeal to many listeners who aren't already true believers.

This is, noted Peacock, a mighty strange strategy coming from people who say one of their main goals is evangelism. He also wonders if it does believers much good to consume only "positive" messages that please them, comfort them and appeal to what marketers call their "felt needs."

Some critics go even further. Writing in The New York Times, critic Nicholas Dawidoff said CCM is simply "mediocre stuff, diluted by hesitation and dogmatic formula, inferior to the mainstream popular music it emulates." But he added, "There's no reason why contemporary Christian performers, if they allow themselves to explore their talent and emotion more completely, can't successfully combine virtuosity and moral virtue."

Mark Joseph of the MJM Entertainment Group in Southern California has dug into sports history and found an even more provocative judgment. "As with baseball, strange bedfellows have colluded to keep musicians with Christian beliefs in the modern-day equivalent of the Negro Leagues," he wrote in Billboard. This arrangement allows Christian companies to lock up their artists, while the biases of the secular marketplace remain unchallenged.

On the other side, some purists say CCM is soul sick because its artists crave mainstream success and respect. This camp claims that it's time to return to a strict "ministry" model in which performers stick to the biblical basics — recording only explicitly Christian songs — and stop seeking to "cross over" into secular charts.

The bottom line, said Peacock, is that gifted Christians make all kinds of music — from classical to jazz, from pop to edgy rock — and it doesn't help anyone to enforce one narrow definition of "Christian music." People who run CCM companies must learn to reach the ears of unbelievers as well as believers, he said. This will, at the very least, require radically different marketing techniques and a more real-life-oriented approach to lyrics.

This would even allow some Christians to successfully write songs that appeal to non-Christians, even if that breaks the CCM rules and might, in the short run, seem unprofitable.

After all, noted Peacock, "an audience of 100 Satan punks and 10 Christians does not constitute a CCM consumer base. An audience of 95 Christians and five Satan punks does. If you're thinking something doesn't add up, you're right. Whether it adds up or not depends on whose math you're using."

THE ROCK FOR LIFE PLEDGE

January 2002

WASHINGTON — The music was angry and ragged, sounding something like a chainsaw gashing a concrete block — only with a beat that bounced the teens up and down.

But this was not the usual mosh scene. This was a Rock for Life concert.

"It seems too easy, unwanted baby, it could just be thrown away," chanted Mike Middleton of a Wisconsin band called Hangnail. "A life so helpless counted as useless, another victim of mankind. . . . Did you even have a name or could you've been like me the same? I was wondering, do they think of you or try to keep you from their minds?"

Not far from the stage was a table lined with stacks of black sweatshirts and T-shirts that are guaranteed to stand out among the Tommy Hilfiger and Abercrombie & Fitch clones in school hallways. The slogans are printed in large white letters and are easy to read, even from a distance.

Some people like that. Some people don't.

"ABORTION IS HOMICIDE," says one sweatshirt. "ABORTION IS MEAN," says another. On the back is a pledge that proclaims: "You will not silence my message. You will not mock my God. You will stop killing my generation." The Rock for Life logo is a cartoon image of an unborn child playing an electric guitar.

The American Life League reported selling 15,000 of the shirts at rallies last summer and at least another 500 during concerts supporting the 2002 March for Life, the 29th anniversary of the U.S. Supreme Court's Roe v. Wade decision.

These shirts will be coming soon to a public school near you if Rock for Life has its way.

"People will probably think that we're weird or something, but we're used to that," said 16-year-old Katie Hammond of Frederick (Md.) High School, not far outside the Washington Beltway. "Sometimes we end up in arguments at lunch about stuff like this. People keep saying, 'It's wrong to believe what you believe' and blah, blah, blah. Maybe it'll be OK."

Then again, there's always a chance someone will freak out and call a counselor. Rock for Life has received a dozen or more complaints about students being sent home for wearing the "ABORTION IS HOMICIDE" shirt. Few have dared to fight these bans. These are tense times on the free-speech front.

"I know some of the schools have a zero-tolerance policy on language about death, so people are saying that the word "homicide" violates that," said the Rev. Patrick Mahoney of the Christian Defense Coalition. "But that just doesn't wash, since you have all kinds of kids walking the halls in T-shirts for rock groups like Slayer, Megadeth and who knows what all. There was even an anti-gun campaign a few years ago with the slogan, 'Stop the killing.' I didn't hear anything about schools banning those shirts.

"So from my point of view, this isn't about the word 'homicide.' What this is about is the word 'abortion.'"

Then there is that dangerous word "God."

In Malone, N.Y., a school attorney claimed the sweatshirt pledge proved that "the student's objective is to proselytize." But such a ban would appear to clash with 1999 Clinton White House guidelines that were backed by a broad coalition ranging from the National Association of Evangelicals to the American Civil Liberties Union. That letter said, "Schools may not single out religious attire in general, or attire of a particular religion, for prohibition or regulation."

Apparently, many Americans are tense and hypersensitive right now about anything that has to do with strong faith or claims of religious truth, said Erik Whittington of Rock for Life. Thus, some want to nip conflict in the bud, even if that means undercutting free speech.

"We had our largest cluster of complaints about the sweatshirts right after Sept. 11 — just a few days or a week after that," he said, moments before one of the Capitol Hill concerts. "There has to be a connection. . . . I think the logic goes like this: pro-life equals right wing, Christian, fanatic, the enemy. Some people think we're the American Taliban."

ELVIS: A PRODIGAL SON?

August 2002

As the woman reached the stage, the musicians behind Elvis Presley could see that she was carrying a crown on a plush pillow.

"It's for you," she said. "You're the king."

Gospel superstar J.D. Sumner recalled that Presley took her hand that night in Las Vegas and replied: "No, honey, I'm not the king. Christ is the king. I'm just a singer."

Anyone digging through the mud of Presley's sad decline can find many signs that he was crying out to God as well as wrestling with his demons. Like many Southern sinners, Elvis did more than his share of Sunday morning weeping while trying to shake off the shame of Saturday night.

So was Elvis a backsliding believer or a hypocritical satyr? A quarter century after his death, it's amazing that Presley can still get people all shook up in churches as well as casinos.

"To judge from some media coverage, you'd think Presley was a saint — a role model to emulate," said evangelical activist Charles Colson in a radio commentary. In their stories about Graceland pilgrims flocking to Memphis, what the journalists "neglected to mention was that, even though Elvis took much of his style from gospel sources, his primary message was the antithesis of biblical standards."

Colson noted that one ABC News clip showed "Elvis singing, 'To spend one night with you is what I pray for.' Wow! Did he really think God answered prayers to expedite one-night stands?"

The final verdict: "Elvis is an object lesson in the wages of sin."

No one would deny that Presley started a cultural earthquake, said Christian radio veteran Dave Fisher, who wrote Colson's BreakPoint.org radio script. The crucial issue is whether "his impact on our culture was uplifting or degrading."

Yes, Presley honored his mother by singing "Precious Lord, Take My Hand" on the "Ed Sullivan Show." But he also helped inspire a cultural and sexual revolution, said Fisher. "Just analyze the lyrics of the songs. . . . Many were quite sexual. He wasn't using the four-letter words that a lot of singers and bands today would use. But they were still suggestive. He opened the door for what was to come."

What about that gospel side of Presley? It's true that he wandered in the wilderness of sex, drugs and rock 'n' roll, said Steve Beard, creator of www.Thunderstruck.org, a Web site on faith and popular culture. It's also true that Elvis was an "eccentric religious seeker on turbodrive," soaking up Hinduism, numerology, transcendental meditation, Buddhism, theosophy and whatever else caught fire in the 1960s.

But as his health failed, Presley's longtime confidant Rick Stanley — who later became a Baptist evangelist — remembers the singer saying Christian prayers of repentance. Only hours before his death, Stanley said he heard Elvis pray: "Dear Lord, please show me a way. I'm tired and confused, and I need your help."

No picture of Elvis is complete without faith, as well as failure. He was not the first or the last devout country boy to stray in the big city.

"If Elvis was a prodigal son, then it seems that he died on the way back to his Father's house," said Beard. "That's tragic. That's a tragic story, and it's a story that ought to inspire compassion, not condemnation. . . . We all need to be reminded that mercy and grace are still Christian virtues."

If there is a cautionary tale here, it is another reminder that believers should be careful when dealing with heroes, said scholar Gene Edward Veith, co-author of "Honky-Tonk Gospel: The Story of Sin and Salvation in Country Music." The lives of celebrities are often full of mixed blessings.

The boy who made his profession of faith in a Baptist church in Tupelo, Miss., struggled to hold on to that faith for the rest of his life. The Elvis story is packed with pain, piety, sin, struggle, glory, guilt and repentance.

"Very few artistic people make good role models," said Veith. "That isn't what artists are about. The conflicts that make them great in the first place are the very same conflicts that would make them bad role models. . . . It's the paradoxes we see in Elvis that made him the great artist that he was."

RICH MULLINS:
ENIGMATIC, RESTLESS, CATHOLIC

May 1998

Father Matt McGinness had never heard the song playing on his car radio, even though "Sing Your Praise to the Lord" was one of superstar Amy Grant's biggest hits.

"Gosh, I really like that song," the priest told a musician friend that night back in 1995. "Well, thanks," responded Rich Mullins. This mystified the priest, who asked what he meant. "I wrote that," said Mullins.

McGinness hadn't realized that Mullins was that famous. The priest simply knew him as another seeker who kept asking questions about doctrine, history and art and was developing a unique spiritual bond with St. Francis of Assisi. At the time of his death in a Sept. 19 car crash, Mullins was taking the final steps to enter Catholicism.

"Rich had made up his mind, and he wasn't hiding anymore," said McGinness, chaplain of the Newman Center at Wichita State University. "But I really don't think it's fair to make him the poster child for Catholic converts. . . . The key to Rich is that he was searching for a deep, lasting unity with God. He was such a reflective man, and that quality brought him both peace and a great deal of anxiety."

Even friends described Mullins as enigmatic and eccentric, and there was much more to him than hit songs, led by the youth-rally anthem "Awesome God." Grant summed up his legacy during last month's Dove Awards in Nashville, in which Mullins received his first Artist of the Year award.

"Rich Mullins was the uneasy conscience of Christian music," she said. "He didn't live like a star. He'd taken a vow of poverty so that what he earned could be used to help others."

McGinness said Mullins often said he felt called to a life of chastity and service, while staying active in music. It was hard to predict his future. His final recordings are slated for release on June 30 as "The Jesus Record."

"Rich didn't know for sure if he was called to ministry, which in the Catholic context would be the priesthood," said McGinness. "He also feared that converting to Catholicism could mean losing his audience. . . . He knew there might be rough days ahead."

It's crucial to remember that Mullins grew up surrounded by fiercely independent brands of Protestantism such as the Quakers and the Churches of Christ, said his brother David Mullins, minister at the Oak Grove Christian Church in Beckley, W.Va. This taught him to fear formality and hierarchies, while also yearning for a faith that united people in all times and places — with no labels.

"Rich had a very low view of church structures, but he had very high ideals about what the church could be," said his brother. "He was sincerely drawn to Catholicism, but he also wondered where he would fit in the Roman Catholic Church."

Nevertheless, Mullins' recent music was steeped in Catholicism, from his autobiographical album "A Liturgy, a Legacy and a Raga-muffin Band" to his "Canticle of the Plains" musical about a Kansas cowboy he called St. Frank. His greatest-hits set was filled with photos of Celtic churches, crucifixes, nuns and statues of Mary. He quoted G.K. Chesterton and Flannery O'Connor, defended the pope and told one interviewer: "I think that a lot of Protestants think that Pentecost happened and then the church disappeared until the Reformation. So there is this long span of time when there was no church. That can't be if Jesus was telling the truth."

After playing telephone tag for a week, McGinness and Mullins talked one last time the night before the fatal accident. Mullins was going to Mass weekly, if not more often. He was ready to say his first confession and be confirmed. They set a meeting in two days. Others said Mullins was aiming for Oct. 4, the Feast of St. Francis.

"There was a sense of urgency," said the priest. "He told me, 'This may sound strange, but I HAVE to receive the body and blood of Christ.' I told him, 'That doesn't sound strange at all. That sounds wonderful.' . . . Of course, I'll always remember that conversation. Rich finally sounded like he was at peace with his decision."

SONGS FOR SOULS IN HARD TIMES

November 2001

The powers that be made sure the Country Music Association Awards started with fireworks, red-white-and-blue streamers and star-spangled guitars.

But it was Alan Jackson who stopped the show with a post-Sept. 11 anthem that had the faithful drying their eyes. "Where Were You (When the World Stopped Turning)" jumped from pangs of doubt to hugs in pews, from tuning out Hollywood trash to dusting off the family Bible.

The man in the white hat wrapped his grief and grit around a chorus that would turn an MTV programmer into a pillar of salt.

"I'm just a singer of simple songs. I'm not a real political man. I watch CNN, but I'm not really sure I can tell you the difference in Iraq and Iran," sang Jackson. "But I know Jesus and I talk to God and I remember this from when I was young. Faith, hope and love are some good things he gave us, and the greatest of these is love."

No one really needed to prove that real country music could

handle hard times. After all, the year's hot song was a 1913 flashback that opens with the cry: "I am a man of constant sorrow, I have seen trouble all my days."

"Country music goes through cycles like everything else, and we've seen a lot of sanitized music in recent years," said Gene Edward Veith of Concordia University-Wisconsin, co-author of "Honky-Tonk Gospel."

"Right now the pendulum is swinging back toward the traditional side of things. That means we're hearing more music that — one way or another — says suffering is a part of real life. This is music about living and dying and joy and sorrow. When you start talking about things like that out in normal America, you have to use the language of faith."

Some people say traditional folk music kept the flame of old-time music alive, while others credit the late Bill Monroe and his bluegrass believers. There's blues, tin-pan jazz and English balladry in there, too. But most of all, said Veith, there is the gospel music that serves as a backdrop to everything else.

Country music is about people messing up and then trying to make things right — sin and salvation. American popular culture knows how to handle the sin part, said Veith. But most of the people who rule Hollywood and the pop charts haven't got a clue about how to handle repentance, grace and salvation.

At its best, country music delivers both sides of this sobering equation.

"Christianity is not a matter of moralism or positive messages," wrote Veith and Thomas Wilmeth. "Rather, it is about the salvation of people who need salvation. Country music, unlike other popular art forms, has a way of acknowledging the sinfulness of sin. And though it sometimes goes too far in wallowing in that sin, at some point it has a way of acknowledging the power of the Gospel."

Country music does do its share of wallowing as well as worshipping. Anyone who has punched more than two jukebox buttons knows that country musicians have always had as much to say about Saturday night as Sunday morning. But even those "cheatin' and drinkin'" songs tend to reveal some moral roots, said Veith.

Many a barstool classic has included a big role for a real Satan who tempts real people with real sin that leads to a real hell. Also, country songs often portray alcohol as a futile way of dealing with moral failure. One thing this music almost never does is deny that the pain and brokenness are real. Meanwhile, it's hard to imagine many rock 'n' roll divas singing songs about adultery, because the institution of marriage is irrelevant in that context.

Country music isn't perfect, said Veith. Neither is real life.

Perhaps Johnny Cash put it best when he described his taste in music: "I love songs about horses, railroads, land, judgment day, family, hard times, whiskey, courtship, marriage, adultery, separation, murder, war, prison, rambling, damnation, home, salvation, death, pride, humor, piety, rebellion, patriotism, larceny, determination, tragedy, rowdiness, heartbreak and love. And mother. And God."

That covers most of the big issues — from Genesis to Revelation.

BLEEPING BAPTISTS PRAY FOR BLEEPING OZZY

January 2003

British tabloid veteran Dan Wooding knows a good headline when he hears one.

Here's a good one for grocery checkout racks: "Churches Pray for the Osbournes." Or even better: "Bleeping Baptists Asked to Pray for the Bleeping Osbournes."

That second headline is true, minus the "bleeping" parts.

The media juggernaut led by Ozzy "The Prince of Darkness" Osbourne and his wife, Sharon, is back in the news, with Mom and Dad renewing their marriage vows before a flock of family, friends and the 1970s disco group Village People. The 20th anniversary rites were delayed several months by Sharon Osbourne's life-and-death struggle with colon cancer.

All of this is, of course, fodder for the hit "reality TV" series about life in the family's Beverly Hills mansion.

"I was watching their show, and I thought to myself: We should have Ozzy Osbourne day in churches across America," said Wooding, now a California-based writer for Christian radio and news. "I mean, these are some people who truly need our prayers."

So Wooding wrote a commentary for the Baptist Press wire service and others asking why Christians don't try praying for distressed entertainers, instead of just cursing them.

Wooding wasn't joking, in large part because his own life once veered into the media wonderland occupied by MTV's First Dysfunctional Family. He was born into a missionary family in Nigeria but raised in Birmingham, England. As a young man, Wooding worked on the warped side of journalism, serving as London correspondent for the National Enquirer, the Sunday Mirror and the Fleet Street tabloids. He chased the Beatles, Monty Python, gangsters, movie stars and everybody else.

It was in 1980 that Wooding — drunk in London's Stab in the Back pub — hit bottom and vowed to return to the faith. He changed gigs but also retained his intense interest in entertainment.

"Christians are so QUICK to judge and write people off as lost causes," he said. "The end result is that the only image of Christianity that someone like Ozzy may ever have is angry protestors marching around outside his shows. . . . Christians need some option other than pointing a finger at people and yelling."

There is evidence, said Wooding, that Ozzy Osbourne is aware of his own "spiritual desperation," which is symbolized by the myriad crosses in his wardrobe and home décor. Ozzy has had private talks about faith with superstar keyboardist Rick Wakeman of Yes, who is also one of Wooding's close friends.

And, as Sharon Osbourne told journalists when their MTV series first hit cable: "The best neighbor we've ever had is Pat Boone. We miss him terribly." Of course, that meant the born-again Boone was on one side and cleaned-up rocker Meat Loaf was on the other, daughter Kelly reminded her mother.

"It was," quipped Ozzy, "sort of like a Satan sandwich."

That's funny, and so is the family's show. But there is also an undercurrent of unhappiness and pain — with the children trashing each other, Ozzy living in a daze and Sharon waging war against the "next-door neighbors from hell," said Wooding.

What is clear to even the most casual viewer is that whatever peace and stability the clan enjoys is rooted in Ozzy and Sharon's marriage and, especially, in her commitment to support him during his legendary struggles with alcohol, aging, depression and the other forms of madness that accompany heavy-metal super-stardom.

"If she goes, I can't even imagine what happens to that man and those children," said Wooding. "So right there, that is something people can pray about. This mother is holding this family together, and she has cancer. Pray for her."

In a way, the Osbourne family can serve as a wake-up call for church people who tend to focus only on life in their own sacred circles, he said.

"The Osbournes are not, believe it or not, the most dysfunctional family in America," he concluded. "Millions of families are just as messed up as they are. The Osbournes at least have the courage to admit how messed up they are. The point is that we need to be praying for messed-up families in general, and maybe praying for the Osbournes would help some people realize that."

WORSHIP FOR SALE, WORSHIP FOR SALE

November 2002

In the beginning, there were the Jesus People.

They had long hair and short memories, and they emerged from the 1960s with a unique fusion of evangelical faith and pop culture. They loved fellowship but didn't like frumpy churches. They trusted their feelings, not traditions. They loved the Bible, but not those old hymnals.

So they started writing, performing, recording and selling songs. The Contemporary Christian Music industry was born.

And, lo, the counterculture became a corporate culture, one that was increasingly competitive and relentlessly contemporary, constantly striving to photocopy cultural trends. In the megachurches, the definition of "worship" changed and then kept changing — Sunday after Sunday.

Even though this industry "makes claims for musical diversity among its ranks, it is primarily a reflection of current folk, pop and rock styles," noted veteran pop musician Charlie Peacock, speaking at a conference on "Music and the Church" at Baylor University in Waco, Texas. "Even today's successful modern worship music is composed of these and does not have a distinct style of its own."

The "bandwidth" of worship music today is actually quite narrow, he said, even if black gospel and urban music are included. This reality is especially obvious if the industry's products are contrasted with the dizzying array of church music found around the world and across two millennia of history.

Today, the bottom line is almost always the financial bottom line.

While believers lead the companies that dominate Christian music, secular corporations now own these smaller companies, noted Peacock. Clearly this is shaping the Christian music sold in religious bookstores and mainstream malls. But this corporate culture is also affecting worship and the heart of church life.

"The industry cannot be expected to always have the best interests of the church in mind," Peacock told nearly 500 scholars, musicians, entrepreneurs and clergy. "Christians within the companies may. But the overriding ideology of the system is to serve the shareholder first."

Serving the shareholders means an endless stream of new products, fads and artists — just like in the secular world. The new always vetoes the old, and the ancient saints don't use credit cards or own stock. Thus, CCM is dominated by pop, rock, urban and new worship music. Classical Christian music is below 1 percent on the charts.

Most worship leaders are trying to blend these radically different musical elements, reported pollster George Barna, describing a survey of Protestant worshippers, pastors and worship leaders. Sometimes the easiest solution is to have different services for different audiences — a strategy the Barna Research Group found in three out of four churches.

Thus, the GI Generation attends a different service than the upbeat baby boomers or the mysterious young faithful of Generations X and Y. The result looks something like an FM radio dial.

"What we know about Americans is that we view ourselves first and foremost as consumers," said Barna. "Even when we walk in the doors of our churches, what we tend to do is to wonder, 'How can

I get a good transaction out of this experience?' . . . So, what we know from our research is that Americans have made worship something that primarily we do for ourselves. When is it successful? When we feel good."

And sometimes people feel bad. According to the pastors, only 9 percent of the surveyed churches were experiencing conflict over music. But it's possible to turn those statistics around and note that 90 percent of all church conflicts reported in this study centered on musical issues.

Is peace possible? Peacock concluded that it will be up to ministers and educators to argue that there is more to worship than the niches on CCM sales charts.

The industry can play a valid role in shaping the content of Christian music, he said, even in "contributing to the congregational music of the church. Still, the industry is at the mercy of a consumer with narrow tastes. Until this changes, it can't possibly function as a definitive caretaker and should not be asked to.

"This means that the stewardship of Christian music from the Psalms, to Ambrose, to Bach, to Wesley, to the Fisk Jubilee Singers and more, belongs to the church and the academy."

THE TESTIMONY OF JOHNNY CASH

September 2003

As a veteran of many Billy Graham crusades, Johnny Cash must have known the parable of the drunken airline passenger by heart.

Here's how Graham told this old, old story during his 1985 South Florida crusade.

One day, the evangelist boarded an airplane at the same time as a fat, boisterous drunk who cursed up a storm and even pinched a stewardess. The crew finally wrestled the man to his seat — right in front of Graham. Another passenger leaned over to the man and said he ought to behave. Didn't he know who was behind him?

"You don't say," the man said. Then he turned and loudly said, "Are you Billy Graham? . . . Put her there! Your sermons have sure helped me!"

After the laughter, Graham warmly introduced Cash, who added another punch line.

"I wonder," said Cash, "why he thought about introducing me right after he talked about the rowdy drunk on the airplane."

Yes, Cash knew his role as a missionary to the backsliders.

The man in black was a country kid who embraced his mother's faith, then flung it away, the hell-raiser who got saved and saved and then saved some more. Cash sang about the hope of heaven and the siren songs of hell. Time magazine put it this way: "Here was a man who knew the Commandments because he had broken so many of them."

The gritty details filled 1,500 songs and a lifetime of work in television, movies, books and nights on the road. For years, Cash prowled the stage on amphetamines and wept as he sang "The Old Rugged Cross" — often in the same show.

Things got better after he married June Carter in 1968, a meeting of souls made in heaven but worked out in the flesh under the parental gaze of Ezra and Maybelle Carter. These country-music pioneers not only prayed at Cash's bedside while he kicked drugs, but hung on through years of front-porch Bible study as he walked the line toward redemption.

Cash was in a spiritual war and he knew it. Thus, he constantly quoted Romans 8:13 as his favorite verse: "For if you live according to the sinful nature, you will die; but if by the Spirit you put to death the misdeeds of the body, you will live."

The superstar also knew that millions of people were watching and waiting for him to fall. He lived in that hot spotlight until the day he died.

"I have been a professional entertainer," said Cash at a 1989 Graham crusade in his home state of Arkansas. "My personal life and problems have been widely publicized. There have been things said about me that made people ask, 'Is Johnny Cash really a Christian?'

"Well, I take great comfort in the words of the apostle Paul, who said, 'What I will to do, that I do not practice. But what I hate, that I do.' And he said, 'It is no longer I who do it, but the sin that dwells within me. But who,' he asks, 'will deliver me from this body of death?' And he answers for himself and for me, 'Through Jesus Christ the Lord.'"

The language Cash used in his Graham crusade testimonies was loftier than his style onstage. But the words hit home because Cash knew that his listeners knew he was there, flaws and all. So he talked about his struggles with drugs — past, present and future. He talked about the flaws in his family life. Cash named his idols and his demons and urged others to do the same.

The man in black was on the same Gospel road throughout his life, even when he detoured into the gutter, said Steve Beard, author of the Cash profile in the book "Spiritual Journeys: How Faith Has Influenced 12 Musical Icons."

"This was the real Johnny Cash. I mean, he was trying to do gospel albums, even during the bad times," said Beard. "He told people that the worst thing the drugs did to him was dull his soul and his senses to where he couldn't hear God and experience God the way he could when he was young.

"That's what he really wanted. That's what he kept searching for."

BONO'S CRUSADE ON THE ROAD

June 2001

As lunch ended in the ornate U.S. Senate Foreign Relations Committee conference room, Sen. Jesse Helms struggled to stand and bid farewell to the guest of honor.

Bono stayed at the conservative patriarch's right hand, doing what he could to help. For the photographers, it would have been hard to imagine a stranger image than this delicate dance between the aging senator and the rock superstar.

"You know, I love you," Helms said softly.

The singer gave the 79-year-old Helms a hug. This private session with a circle of senators during this U2 Washington stop wasn't the first time Bono and Helms have discussed poverty, plagues, charity and faith. Nor will it be the last. Blest be the ties that bind.

"What can I say? It's good to be loved — especially by Jesse Helms," Bono said two days later, as his campaign for Third World debt relief continued on Capitol Hill.

The key to this scene is that Bono can quote the Book of Leviticus as well as the works of John Lennon. While his star power opens doors, it is his sincere, if often unconventional, Christian faith that creates bonds with cultural conservatives — in the Vatican and inside the Beltway. Bono has shared prayers and his sunglasses with Pope John Paul II. Don't be surprised if he trades boots and Bible verses with President George W. Bush.

The hot issues right now are red ink and AIDS in Africa. An entire continent is "in flames," said Bono, and millions of lives are at stake. God is watching.

The bottom line is that the Bible contains 2,000 verses about justice and compassion. While it's crucial to answer political and economic questions linked to forgiving $200 billion in Third World debts, Bono said this also must be seen as a crisis of faith. The road into the heart of America runs through its sanctuaries.

"What will really wake people up," he said, "is when Sunday schools start making flags and getting out in the streets. . . . Forget about the judgment of history. For those of you who are religious people, you have to think about the judgment of God."

Bono knows that this bleak, even melodramatic, message sounds bizarre coming from a rock 'n' roll fat cat. In a Harvard University commencement address, he said the only thing worse than an egotistical rock star is a rock star "with a conscience — a placard-waving, knee-jerking, fellow-traveling activist with a Lexus and a swimming pool shaped like his own head."

This is old news to Bono, who has had a love-hate relationship with stardom for two decades. In U2's early days, other Christians said the band should break up or flee into "Christian rock," arguing that fame always corrupts. Bono and his band mates decided otherwise, but the singer soon began speaking out about his faith and his doubts, his joys and his failures.

"I don't believe in preaching at people," he told me back in 1982. A constant theme in his music, he added, is the soul-spinning confusion that results when spirituality, sensuality, ego and sin form a potion that is both intoxicating and toxic. "The truth is that we are all sinners. I always include myself in the 'we.' . . . I'm not telling everybody that I have the answers. I'm trying to get across the difficulty that I have being what I am."

Eventually, Bono acted out this internal debate onstage. In the 1990s, he celebrated and attacked fame through a sleazy, macho, leather-bound alter ego called the Fly. After that came Mister MacPhisto, a devilishly theatrical take on mass-media temptation. The motto for the decade was "Mock Satan, and he will flee thee."

Today, U2 has all but dropped its ironic posturing, and the soaring music of this tour covers sin and redemption, heaven and hell, mercy and grace. Bono is quoting from the Psalms, and the first Washington concert ended with him shouting: "Praise! Unto the Almighty!"

It wasn't subtle and it wasn't perfect. Crusades rarely are.

"I do believe that the kingdom of heaven is taken by force," said Bono, paraphrasing the Gospel of Matthew, chapter 11. "God doesn't mind if we bang on the door to heaven sometimes, asking him to listen to what we have to say. . . . At least, that's the kind of religion I believe in."

BIG IDEAS ON THE BIG SCREEN

Haddon Robinson couldn't believe what he was hearing. He was chatting with a businessman in the next airplane seat, and after Robinson revealed that he was a seminary professor, the man responded with a blunt question: "What is Christmas?"

The businessman had seen all the usual holiday movies. Still, he was confused. For example, what roles did Santa Claus and Jesus play in all of this?

Robinson did his best to explain. The man listened and, instead of changing the subject, asked, "So what is Easter?" That led to, "What do you mean by 'Resurrection'?"

Recounting the story a few years later, Robinson said he tried, in nonthreatening language, to describe the biblical accounts of God raising Jesus from the dead and why this belief was so important.

"Then this man said to me, 'Do all Christians believe that?'

"I said, 'All Christians should believe that.'

"Then he said, 'That's interesting. I think I knew about Christmas. But I didn't really know about Easter.'"

This last statement puzzled Robinson, but later something clicked.

Christmas images, traditions and hymns have made it into pop culture, and everyone hears or sees snippets of the story year after year, even if it has been diluted. But where — via the shopping mall, multiplex and mini-satellite dish — would anyone soak up images, hymns and themes from Easter? For millions of people, the Resurrection is what happens (sort of) in "The Matrix" trilogy. Those are Christian movies, right?

This businessman was an ordinary American. He had consumed decades of visual media, baptizing his imagination in visual images and stories. Television, of course, was the dominant medium, the medium that buzzed and flickered in the background of daily life. But then there were the powerful symbols and stories that he remembered best, and most of them came from movies.

Movies are the books of a culture raised on television.

If missionaries came to America, they would immediately recognize this. They would study the moral and religious messages in visual media, seeking insights into the lives of ordinary Americans.

This is how missionaries think. But this is not how the vast majority of religious leaders think. As a result, few clergy are taught to think like missionaries. Thus, few believers in the pews know how to make sense out of the images and emotions that help define their lives. Still, the movies, and related forms of entertainment, provide what Dr. Quentin Schultze and other communication scholars at Calvin College call the "maps of reality" that guide the mass-media faithful.

Haddon Robinson understands, because he is not your typical seminary professor. He has been studying these issues since the mid-1950s, during his communications doctoral work at the University of Illinois. I knew him as president of Denver Seminary and have continued to teach with him in his preaching seminars in the Doctor of Ministry program at Gordon-Conwell Theological Seminary outside Boston. In 1996, Baylor University named him as one of the top 12 preachers in the English-speaking world.

The key, says Robinson, is that modern religious leaders must "exegete their culture" as well as they exegete God's Word. Preachers and teachers must study the forces that shape the lives of real people. That would mean taking visual media seriously — especially movies. But this is threatening to mainstream religious leaders. Thus, many choose to remain silent, while others rage against the media, seeing only the negative.

What they need to do is think like missionaries.

Pop culture is a warped mirror of our lives, but it is a mirror nonetheless. The goal is to be able to mix criticism of mass media's contents and social role with a sobering realization of the power of mass media in modern life. We must be realistic, critical and, ultimately, constructive.

Meanwhile, Robinson is afraid that too many megachurch leaders have swung to the other extreme, uncritically turning their sanctuaries into movie theaters. Many churches are adding expensive digital equipment and leaping into multimedia music, humor and movie-clip-driven sermons.

Clergy soon discover that they're expected to use this gear every Sunday. The audience demands it, he said.

"The pastor is thinking, 'Now that I have all of this stuff, where can I throw it in?'" Robinson told me. "All of a sudden, rather than thinking of the most effective way to communicate a message, you're thinking about all that money you've spent. . . . You're thinking about media, where before you were thinking about your message."

Robinson's advice to modern preachers is that they worry less about using media and more about studying the impact of the fog of visual images that surround their people. Today, every congregation includes people who understand little or nothing about the Bible or basic doctrines. Their heads and hearts are full of conflicting images and values, the result of years of spiritual channel-surfing.[1]

To one degree or another, it has been true ever since movie theaters became the alternative sanctuary in which ordinary Americans wrestled with the big ideas of life.

We must realize that the church lives in a hostile technological environment, one that "communicates with images," said Robinson in a pivotal 1990 sermon. "It doesn't come out and argue. It just simply shows you pictures, day after day after day after day. Before you realize it, in the basement of your mind, you discover that you have shifted your values, and many times you've lost your faith."[2]

"THE PASSION" OF OLD WORDS AND SYMBOLS

January 2004

Jesuits rarely receive frantic calls from Hollywood megastars rushing to finish movies that are causing media firestorms.

But Father William Fulco is getting used to it, as Mel Gibson completes his cathartic epic "The Passion of the Christ."

While mixing dialogue the other day, Gibson hit a scene in which a man standing at a door lacked something to say. The director needed a line — right now. Fulco's first question was unique to this project: Was this character supposed to speak Latin or first-century Aramaic?

"Mel said the camera was not on the speaker's face, so we did not need to synchronize what he said with the movements of his mouth," said Fulco, who translated the screenplay into the two ancient languages, with English subtitles.

"The character needed to say something in Aramaic in the ballpark of, 'What do you want?' So I had him say in rather colloquial early Aramaic, 'Mah? Mah ba'eh?' That is literally, 'What? What wanting?'"

That worked.

It has been nearly two years since Fulco answered the telephone and heard an unfamiliar voice blurt out: "Hey, Padre! It's Mel!"

Gibson's proposal was unusual, but it fit the Jesuit's skills as a professor of ancient Mediterranean studies at Loyola Marymount University in Los Angeles. Fulco began digging into Hebrew texts seeking the roots of the now-dead Aramaic language, while simultaneously exploring dialects such as Syriac spoken today in tiny Christian enclaves in Iran, Syria and Turkey. He also stepped into heated academic debates between those who favor a more Italian-friendly Latin and those who reject this approach.

"I'm getting hate mail about Latin pronunciations," said Fulco. "One guy wrote who was angry about what he called 'these ecclesiastical bastardizations' of the Latin. Not only was he going to boycott the movie, he said he was going to call his high school Latin teacher and tell her to boycott the movie as well. . . .

"I have to keep reminding people: This is not a documentary. We had to make artistic choices."

Legions of critics, of course, oppose the film for other reasons. Liberal Catholics and some Jewish leaders claim the script is tainted by anti-Semitism. Meanwhile, Gibson — who has invested $25 million in the project — has previewed early versions to rapt audiences of traditional Catholics, evangelicals and others. The film opens on 2,000 U.S. screens on Ash Wednesday.

It is crucial to realize that the images and language at the heart of "The Passion of the Christ" flow directly out of Gibson's personal dedication to Catholicism in one of its most traditional and mysterious forms: the 16th-century Latin Mass.

"I don't go to any other services," the director told the Eternal Word Television Network. "I go to the old Tridentine Rite. That's the way that I first saw it when I was a kid. So I think that that informs one's understanding of how to transcend language. Now, initially, I didn't understand the Latin. . . . But I understood the meaning and the message and what they were doing. I understood it very fully, and it was very moving and emotional and efficacious, if I may say so."

The goal of the movie is to shake modern audiences by brashly juxtaposing the "sacrifice of the cross with the sacrifice of the altar — which is the same thing," said Gibson. This ancient union of symbols and sounds has never lost its hold on him. There is, he stressed, "a lot of power in these dead languages."

Thus, the seemingly bizarre choice of Latin and Aramaic was actually part of the message. The goal of Gibson's multicultural, multilingual team was to make a statement that transcended any one time, culture and tongue.

"We didn't want another movie with Jesus as some kind of Aryan superman or Jesus as a surfer," said Fulco. "We saw one movie in which Jesus was almost this Michael Jackson kind of character. Try to imagine that. . . .

"We didn't want an American Jesus, or a Japanese Jesus or a French Jesus. What we wanted was a language that allowed Jesus to be none of these nationalities, so that he can be all of them at the same time. This is a universal story."

"TITANIC": THE SIXTIES AS SACRAMENTS
March 1998

Soon after "Titanic" opened in the United States, director James Cameron ventured into cyberspace to field questions from waves of stricken fans.

One mother described how her young daughter sat spellbound through the three-hour-plus romance between a first-class girl trapped in a loveless engagement with a cruel fiancé and a starving artist who liberates her, then surrenders his life to save her in the icy North Atlantic. As they left the theater, the mother said her daughter noticed older girls weeping.

"It's OK, don't worry," the child said, giving one girl a hug. "Rose is with her Jack now."

"That's so sweet," wrote Cameron. Nevertheless, he told another participant in the Online Tonight session that he wouldn't answer one common question: Did the now-elderly Rose die in the last scene, to be reunited with her lover aboard the Titanic in a vision of heaven, or was she merely dreaming?

As he immersed himself in Titanic lore, Cameron said he reached one conclusion. "I think I discovered the truth of its lesson — which is all you have is today." In another public statement, he described his film in more sweeping terms. "'Titanic' is not just a cautionary tale — a myth, a parable, a metaphor for the ills of mankind. It is also a story of faith, courage, sacrifice and, above all else, love."

"Titanic" filled a hole in the hearts of millions of romance-starved moviegoers. Whether Cameron intended to or not, Hollywood's most successful movie of all time also has changed how at least one generation views one of this century's most symbolic events.

For millions, "Titanic" is a triumphant story of how one upper-crust girl found salvation — body and soul — through sweaty sex, modern art, self-esteem lingo and social rebellion. "Titanic" is a passion play celebrating the moral values of the 1960s as sacraments. Rose sums it up by saying that she could abandon her old life and family because her forbidden lover "saved me in every way that a person can be saved."

Millions are walking their children down theater aisles, often making many such pilgrimages, in support of this cathartic message about the power of romantic love. Major religious groups that have greeted similar films with howls of protest are silent. A few people wonder why.

"'Titanic' reminds me of the distinctions between people of faith and secularists," said conservative commentator Elizabeth Farah. "While all agree that death is inevitable and very often unexpected, the religious and secularists do not agree on the behavior life's fragility should promote. Those of faith know they may meet their Maker at any moment, at which time they will account for their sins. Their fear and deep love for God inspires them in their constant struggle for righteousness. To the secularist, life is short — get what you want when you want it, and in whatever way necessary."

The heroes of this modern "Titanic" fit into this latter category, said Farah. Their sins become virtues, because they are rebelling against people who are portrayed as even worse. This isn't just a bad movie, she added. It is "manipulative" and "fundamentally immoral."

Father Patrick Henry Reardon, a philosophy professor and Orthodox priest, goes even further in the next issue of the ecumenical journal Touchstone. He calls the movie "satanic." The people who built the Titanic were so proud of their command of technology that they boasted that God couldn't sink their ship. Today, the creators of the movie "Titanic" substitute romantic love as the highest power. Jack becomes Rose's savior, and he does more than save her life.

"Had that been all that happened, I would not have complained," said Reardon. "But they made that Christ symbol into a very attractive antiChrist. The line that set me off I believe also to have been the defining line of the film: the assertion that the sort of saving that Jack did was, ultimately, the only kind of saving possible. If that was the thesis statement of the film, then I start looking for the cloven hoof and sniffing for brimstone."

SIGNALS FROM
HOLLYWOOD HEAVEN

November 1998

It's another day at the mall multiplex, where hip witches are look-ing for love, Oprah is fighting her demons, free will and sin are invading a suburban utopia and vampires are being born again, more or less.

Moviegoers also have the option of going to heaven and hell with superstar Robin Williams in "What Dreams May Come." The big news in this "Hollywood Heaven" opus is that some gatekeepers in America's dream factory are trying to take eternity seriously — per-haps more seriously than most conventional religious leaders.

"This movie wasn't nearly as bad as I thought it would be. It even contains some hopeful signs for those who believe heaven and hell are real," said Boston College philosopher Peter Kreeft, author of 30-plus books, including "Heaven: The Heart's Deepest Longing." In terms of America's growing fascination with spirituality, he added, it's clear that "people are asking some of the right questions, right now. They are spiritually hungry, even if they are choosing to eat poisonous food."

As was the case with "Ghost" and numerous other modern movies in this genre, Kreeft said that "What Dreams May Come" appears to be "essentially a Buddhist or Hindu movie" created for audiences that remain comfortable with Judeo-Christian images. After death, the characters learn that there are no rules that govern eternity, reincarnation is a viable option and reality is a simple mat-ter of perception. "What's true in our minds is true, whether people know it or not," explains one heavenly teacher.

Early on, Williams' Everyman character asks an angelic figure

what role God plays in this dreamlike heaven. "He's up there somewhere, shouting down that he loves us," says the spirit.

An ad for a Los Angeles seminar on "Metaphysical Filmmaking,"
led by producer Stephen Simon, sums up his goals: "As we approach
the new millennium, film is the natural medium for the expression
of transformational consciousness. Metaphysical films can illumi-
nate new landscapes, chart new maps and model new paradigms for
relating to life." The result is part Dante's "Inferno" and part "Star
Trek," served up with waves of special effects and pop psychology.

But it would be wrong to dismiss this as mere New Age propaganda, stressed Kreeft, who is a very traditional Roman Catholic. The
movie focuses on a crucial subject — eternal life — which churches
have all but ignored for at least a generation. And while the doctrine
is unorthodox, it contains images of heaven and hell that are almost
shockingly traditional.

"This movie was gorgeous and fascinating to look at, but there
was more to it than that," he said. "This wasn't a kind of minimalist
kind of beauty. It was opulent. It was an old-fashioned, natural kind
of beauty. That's important. We need to be able to say that heaven
is beautiful."

In addition to affirming the existence of heaven and hell, the
movie shows that decisions in this life impact the life to come. It
teaches that people must not lose faith or let fear dominate their
lives. It stresses the need for courage, forgiveness and gratitude.

Above all, "What Dreams May Come" takes love seriously. This
is, conceded Kreeft, human love, instead of divine love. But at least
the human love depicted in this movie is noble and beautiful. Many
critics have savaged the movie because its depiction of marital love
is based more on idealism than sexual passion.

"This movie did get human love right," said Kreeft. "It showed
love as charity and self-sacrifice. It praises faithfulness . . . and this
love even includes children. There's an intact family, for once, and

we see many beautiful scenes showing the love in this family. That's positive."

There are even scenes of repentance. But everyone repents to each other, not to God.

"They do repent to somebody, which is a start," said Kreeft. "That's better than, 'Love means never having to say you're sorry.' . . . What the movie didn't say, of course, was that God counts and that God judges. It didn't say that one finds true joy by conforming to God's reality. . . . In a way, the movie was simply too spiritual. It didn't take reality seriously enough."

DUVALL ON SWEAT, SIN AND THE SOUTH

March 1998

Most movies about the South look like they were filmed in Southern California.

What's missing are heat, sweat, rust, bugs, mud and another messy reality called "sin." These movies contain sinful behavior, but nobody calls it "sin" or says folks should do anything about it. This is strange, since the real South contains zones in which people still wear Sunday clothes, carry ragged Bibles and say prayers before meals in restaurants.

"Most folks in New York and out here in California just don't know what to do with life below the New Jersey shore," said Robert Duvall, who has spent several weeks doing waves of interviews trying to explain his film "The Apostle" to the media world. "They just can't seem to get it right. . . . Everything ends up looking and sounding all wrong."

Lots of people understand that sinners can do good and that saints don't win all their battles with their demons. It's the people who really believe in sin who understand that sin, repentance and redemption are often messy subjects, said Duvall, who recently received an Oscar nomination for his performance as the flawed but faithful preacher E.F. "Sonny" Dewey.

"There really are preachers in jail. I've met guys like that who have done all kinds of bad things, even murder and rape," said Duvall, who wrote "The Apostle" script in longhand and directed it himself. "These guys are real people, and they struggle with the good and the bad that's in their own souls. They're human. I wanted to show the reality of that struggle. . . . My guy makes mistakes. But he's more good than bad. He hangs on to his faith, because it's real."

Duvall's Pentecostal preacher sums it all up one night in a showdown with God, just after losing his wife and church to a younger preacher. "I love you, Lord. I love you, but I am mad at you!" he shouts. "I know I'm a sinner, every once in a while, and a womanizer. But I'm your servant. I have been ever since I was a little boy and you brought me back from the dead."

A few scenes later, he bashes his rival with a baseball bat in a fatal flash of rage and then flees. He's the kind of man who shouts "Glory! Glory!" as he sinks his getaway car into muddy waters and then rebaptizes himself as a reborn apostle. He defends his new interracial church with his fists, while the people sing, "There's wonder-working power in the blood." As he gives a final altar call, with police-car lights flashing in the church parking lot, he tells a convert: "I'm going to jail and you're going to heaven. . . . Glory be to God on high."

This character's roots run back 25 years, to a time when Duvall began visiting a church in Arkansas while doing research. He wrote the script in 1984 and spent 13 years wrestling with Hollywood's principalities and powers, trying to get it on film. Finally, he invested $5 million of his own money. Many of the people in the movie weren't acting, including a Pentecostal pastor who fasted for 24 hours before going on camera. Duvall is the star, but it's easy to spot the real preachers. Their voices soar, while the director often has the good sense to just stand and watch.

Meanwhile, Duvall is getting used to answering questions about his own faith. The son of a Methodist father and a Christian Scientist mother, he calls himself a believer, even if others on the Gospel road might consider parts of his life unconventional. The key, said Duvall, is that he respects the role faith plays in the lives of millions of Pentecostal and fundamentalist believers, even if these people scare the living daylights out of Hollywood.

"A lot of the people who are praising this movie would never set foot inside one of these churches," he said. "They tell me, 'These people frighten me.' And I say, 'Why? These are good, moral people. You'd be in a lot more danger walking around in parts of New York City than you would be hanging out in these kinds of churches.'"

THE LATE GREAT PLANET HOLLYWOOD
February 2001

The book was a global phenomenon and inspired sequel after sequel until millions rallied around the apocalyptic cry, "Don't be left behind!"

True believers handed copies to friends and warned strangers about the Second Coming. Evangelists said the books would convict sinners. It would have made a great movie, except that William E. Blackstone's "Jesus Is Coming" came out in 1878, before Hollywood was born.

"These books were very, very popular. . . . They gave evangelists a new weapon in the war for souls," said Baptist historian Timothy Weber, author of "Living in the Shadow of the Second Coming: American Premillennialism, 1875-1982."

"If you read the sermons from back then, it's clear that the great revival preachers were using the same kinds of lines. They were saying, 'Christ could return before I finish this very sentence! Are you ready? What will happen to you if your loved ones vanish into heaven?' . . . You heard this all across America. They were saying, 'Don't be left behind!'"

These apocalyptic visions are alive and well, as the thriller "Left Behind" by Tim LaHaye and Jerry B. Jenkins leaps from mall bookstores into movie theaters. The first eight books in the planned 12-book opus have sold 25 million copies, with audio and kids' editions selling 11 million more.

The movie — produced for a mere $17 million — blends snippets of "Independence Day" warfare and Bible-conference plot twists. Secular critics are slamming it, with the Washington Post calling the film a "blundering cringefest." Some Christians have cautiously called it a small step forward for religious entertainment. Truth is, parts of "Left Behind: The Movie" are so bad it could become a hip classic, a fundamentalist "Rocky Horror Picture Show."

One thing is certain: The 700 churches and businesses that invested $3,000 each to help Cloud Ten Pictures distribute the movie did so in an attempt to win converts.

Belief in the second coming of Christ is an ancient doctrine. But in the 19th century, John Nelson Darby, Blackstone and other "premillennial dispensationalists" began dividing world history into a complicated series of covenants and "dispensations." They believed

Jesus would "rapture" believers up into heaven before a seven-year time of tribulation, followed by an apocalyptic battle between good and evil and Christ's victorious return. This "rapture" concept was especially popular with evangelists.

"Until then," explained Weber, "all preachers really had was the threat of unexpected death, the whole idea of asking, 'If you died tonight, would you be ready to meet God?' Well, that's serious business, but people get used to the idea that they might die. . . . The idea of a mysterious, secret rapture took things to a completely different level. How do you debate that?"

After grasping this central image, many converts graduate into a labyrinthine school of prophecy built on highly literal interpretations of the Books of Revelation and Daniel and other mysterious Bible passages. This approach infuriates traditional scholars, yet has long intrigued spiritual seekers — especially in the age of mass media and paperback theology. In the 1970s, Hal Lindsey and Carole C. Carlson built a publishing empire on "The Late Great Planet Earth," one of the biggest nonfiction hits of that decade.

Dispensationalism has it all. It offers a doctrinal system that claims to address everything from Y2K to OPEC, from Darwin to the United Nations, from Russian nuclear strategy to how many Israeli jets can land on the head of a pin. It also packs an emotional punch. Adults raised in homes steeped in this worldview always have childhood stories to tell about frightening moments when they asked: "Where is everybody? Have I been left behind?"

These images make sense when fleshed out in sermons and books that provide lengthy passages to explain complicated historical references and obscure symbols. But outsiders will struggle to read between the pictures in "Left Behind: The Movie."

"This may turn into a tribal ritual for people who have already bought into this whole system" of beliefs, said Weber. "You have to wonder if this movie will work as evangelism, in this day and age.

. . . There's going to be a lot of head scratching going on out there in movie theaters."

A HAIL MARY FOR HOLLYWOOD

February 2003

In the Hollywood culture wars, Barbara Nicolosi is an army of one, a former nun turned screenwriter who constantly urges angry believers to love the artists who so frequently mock them.

"How many of you have complained — or been enraged even — in the last month by something you have seen on television or in a movie theater?" she asked an audience in Los Angeles.

Hundreds of hands went up.

Nicolosi gently pounced: "Now, how many of you, when you saw that something on the screen that offended you, paused and said a prayer for the filmmakers or producers behind that production?"

Two or three hands were raised — slowly.

This is part of the problem, she said. The entertainment industry needs diversity. It needs new talent, viewpoints, passion and stories. But a creative sea change will not occur until churches grasp Hollywood's importance in American and global culture and, yes, even begin praying about it.

Most of the time, Nicolosi speaks to flocks of evangelicals on behalf of a national educational project she leads called Act One: Writing for Hollywood. But on this day she was facing members of Legatus, a network of Catholic CEOs and philanthropists.

This allowed Nicolosi to do something she said she had long wanted to do but lacked the right forum. Bowing her head, she asked the Catholics gathered before her to focus on the Hollywood community and then join her as she said: "Hail Mary, full of grace, the Lord is with thee. Blessed art thou amongst women and blessed is the fruit of thy womb, Jesus. . . ."

Nicolosi plays a unique role, but she is not alone. She is part of a growing nondenominational effort to convince schools and ministries to get serious about creating real entertainment for real audiences, instead of cranking out Christian products that preach to the choir. Her passion for this cause began while working at Paulist Productions with the late Father Ellwood "Bud" Kieser, who was best known for making the movie "Romero" and years of "Insight" television programs.

Someone had to read the large stacks of scripts offered by Christians convinced that God had inspired their work. That sad person was Nicolosi. All but a few of these efforts, she said, dryly, were "badly written, banal, on the nose, pedantic schlock."

For some reason, most of Hollywood's critics think that because movies are easy to watch, they must be easy to make. Thus, tiny squads of true believers — with no experience and little training — keep attempting mission impossible.

"We think we're going to raise $5 million and make a movie about St. John Chrysostom, and suddenly people are going to fall down on their knees all over the world and Jesus will float down from heaven on a cloud," said Nicolosi.

This isn't how Hollywood works. It is a town that is fiercely committed to excellence, and its high-stakes projects require teamwork and compromise by almost everyone involved, she said. It is a town fueled by unbelievable amounts of pressure, power, paranoia and agonizing moral choices.

The way to prepare to enter this arena is to learn from professionals who already thrive there. This is why Act One's seminars are taught by a team of 75 Christians with credits in shows ranging from "MASH" to "Buffy the Vampire Slayer," from "Braveheart" to

"X-Men." The screenwriting program (www.actoneprogram.com) is based at Hollywood Presbyterian Church but will soon become independent and take on new topics, such as directing and producing.

Hollywood's critics need to get serious, or they will continue to look foolish, said Nicolosi.

"There is a sense of outrage in many Christians that the industry should instinctively know how to make the movies that we want to see, and should make them," she said. "That is ridiculous. They are making the movies that THEY want to see, which is their right. . . . Just suppose that the situation were reversed, and we were the ones who had all of the cultural power in our hands. Would we feel obligated to make a few disgusting films for those groups of perverted folks out there to enjoy, just to be fair?

"Of course not. We have to stop begging and whining."

SHOULD A CHRISTIAN DO A NUDE SCENE?
November 1999

One by one, the summer flicks have faded from theater screens, entering the brief purgatory that precedes rebirth on video and cable television.

Most are forgotten sooner rather than later.

"The Thomas Crown Affair" was one typical piece of Hollywood eye candy, focusing on a filthy-rich hunk who commits crimes as a hobby and the femme fatale who stalks him. This was not the kind of movie that normally inspires discussions in a seminary or in churches.

Then again, this steamy thriller featured a star-turn performance by 40-something actress Rene Russo, a born-again Christian who bared both her emotions and her body. It raised serious issues for believers who frequent pews and Bible studies in Hollywood.

"I see no sign that the questions she raised are going to go away anytime soon," said evangelical theologian Robert Johnston, who teaches the "Theology and Film" course at Fuller Theological Seminary in Pasadena, Calif. "Movie people always have a lot to talk about when they get together to discuss the issues that affect Christians who work in this town. But it seems like somebody always asks, 'Would you ever do a nude scene?' It's such a symbolic question."

Russo faced this agonizing issue during promotional interviews, explaining that she spent hours in prayer and turned to a therapist. She discussed her role as wife and mother. She described her charismatic, slain-in-the-Holy-Spirit conversion as a teen and her return to faith as an adult in Bible classes at the famous Church on the Way in Van Nuys.

The ultimate issue, she said, was not nudity. "I don't know where in the Bible it says, 'Don't be nude in a motion picture,'" she told Los Angeles Magazine. The question was whether she should, as a Christian, accept the challenge of playing a fictional character who is amoral, manipulative and, at times, plain old nasty.

"It was like, whoa, this is a woman who totally leads with her sex," said Russo. "Here is a character who is European. She doesn't know if she has her top on or not. She doesn't care. She is a different kind of woman, and it's not who I am. And it was really scary for me."

This line of defense only raises more questions. Would her critics have approved if she played the same amoral, sexy character yet managed to keep more of her clothes on? Why?

What if she played the same role but allowed the use of an anonymous "body double" to take her place in nude scenes?

Or how about this somewhat theoretical question: What if a Hollywood director asked Russo to play a loving wife, shown in

a romantic nude scene with an actor playing the role of her hus-
band, in a film that defended faith and virtue? Was nudity acceptable
in the wedding-night scene in "Braveheart"?

Meanwhile, asked Johnston, why aren't moral conservatives asking
as many tough questions about roles that involve other deadly sins?
Can Christian artists depict war criminals, tyrants, bigots and crooks?
Should a Christian actress think twice about playing Lady Macbeth?

This behavior issue leads to another question: If it is wrong for
religious believers to play these kinds of characters, especially in
nude scenes, is it just as wrong for other religious believers to watch
these entertaining images in theaters or at home?

"We get so upset about issues of nudity and sex in art and entertainment, while issues of violence and killing don't seem to bother us as
much," he said. "We Protestants, in particular, have a special problem
with body and with images of the body. This affects painting and dance
and theater, as well. . . . Meanwhile, Rene Russo is right on target when
she said that the real question was the behavior of her character."

The actress admitted that her choice raised disturbing questions.
She told USA Today that she soon developed a spiritual answer for
this essentially spiritual question.

"Did I do the right thing?" asked Russo. "I always say to Christians
who say I'm wrong, 'Well, you know what? Pray for me. Just pray
for me.'"

MISSION? FILLING IN SOME "HOLES"

April 2003

Look up *mission* in a dictionary, and it's clear why the word makes
Hollywood nervous.

A "mission" can be "an aim in life, arising from a conviction or sense of calling." That's nice and secular. But what if "mission" means "a group set apart by a church or other religious organization to make conversions"?

So film insiders flinch when a studio's mission statement proclaims: "Walden Media believes that quality entertainment is inherently educational. We believe that by providing children, parents and educators with a wide range of great entertainment . . . we can recapture young imaginations, rekindle curiosity and demonstrate the rewards of knowledge and virtue."

Say what? When a studio starts combining words such as "parents" and "virtue," Hollywood folks assume all its movies will start with a roar from Dr. James Dobson, instead of a lion. Wait, isn't that William "Book of Virtues" Bennett atop the Walden advisory committee?

"Our goal is wholesome, uplifting, family-friendly entertainment that is still competitive in the marketplace," said the Rev. Bob Beltz, director of special media projects for billionaire investor Philip Anschutz. "I'm not going to say that all of our films will be faith-based. But I can say that we hope they will all be faith-friendly. . . .

"We want to be a positive influence in Hollywood. But we have to sell tickets to do that."

Take "Holes," for example, which features Louis Sachar's screenplay based on his Newberry Medal-winning novel. The movie opened on 2,331 screens and soared toward $20 million at the box office.

"In a time when mainstream action is rigidly contained within formulas," noted critic Roger Ebert, "maybe there's more freedom to be found in a young people's adventure. 'Holes' jumps the rails, leaves all expectations behind and tells a story that's not funny ha-ha but funny peculiar."

Amen, said Beltz. This story does have a strange, edgy "parable-like feel to it," he said. But it is the movie's serious themes of good and evil, hope and despair, grace and judgment that are catching viewers off guard. Still, while "Holes" contains many religious themes and symbols, it never resorts to preaching. That made it perfect for this new studio.

"When you have a story like that, you don't want to add anything to it or take anything away," he said. "You just want the story to speak for itself."

Millions of American students already know about Stanley Yelnats IV, a good kid who ends up in the wrong place at the right time and is sentenced to dig holes at the hellish Camp Green Lake in West Texas. The lake is dry, and the lovely town on the shore is long dead. But there are serpents, scorpions, killer lizards, bitter memories, buried secrets and enough shame to cover everybody. The sins of the fathers are literally being visited upon the sons.

On one level, "Holes" revolves around a gypsy fortuneteller's curse on Stanley's "no-good-dirty-rotten-pig-stealing-great-great-grand-father." But the emotional heart of this multigenerational tale is the divine judgment that hangs over Green Lake. The town's elite once killed an innocent black onion-picker for the crime of falling in love with a white schoolteacher.

The book spells out what the movie acts out: "That all happened 110 years ago. Since then, not one drop of rain has fallen on Green Lake. You make the decision: Whom did God punish?"

In the end, the guilty are brought to justice, the innocent go free and the curses are lifted. Stanley and his friends dance as life-giving water pours from the sky onto the parched earth. The big question: Who can make it rain?

Viewers can make up their own minds about that, said educator Michael Flaherty, the president of Walden Media. But if movies are good enough, many will want to dig deeper.

"Many companies that set out to produce family entertainment make the mistake of defining themselves in terms of what they are not going to do," he said. "They say, 'Don't worry. We're not going to have any bad language in our movies.' Or they say, 'Don't worry. Our stories won't have all those bad parts.'

"We think we can do better than that. We think we can make high-quality films and still be true to our mission."

A CHICK FLICK TO REMEMBER

February 2002

No one was surprised when "A Walk to Remember" opened and drew flocks of teenage girls to the suburban supercinemas that circle America's biggest cities.

This was, after all, a multihankie chick flick staring pop diva Mandy Moore. After a week, it was the No. 3 movie and had pulled in $12.2 million, which raised some Hollywood eyebrows because it only cost about $10 million to make.

Then the plot thickened. In weeks two and three, ticket sales hit $23.3 and then $30.3 million. "A Walk to Remember" was doing OK in major cities but soaring in smaller cities and towns across the heartland. Was the quiet little romance about a chaste preacher's daughter and a brooding troublemaker reaching a new demographic?

"We don't want to go out to theater lobbies and ask people, 'Are you a born-again Christian? Are you going to recommend this movie to people at your church?' But it seems clear this movie is attracting people who normally don't dash out to movie theaters," said veteran producer Denise Di Novi. "We must be getting good word-of-mouth support from people who are saying, 'This is not a typical Hollywood teen movie. You can trust this one.'"

"A Walk to Remember" began with a novel by Nicholas Sparks,

an active Catholic. The movie tells the story of Jamie Sullivan, the devout but spunky daughter of a small-town Baptist pastor, and Landon Carter, a handsome jerk in need of redemption. Jamie carries a Bible, helps poor children, dresses modestly, obeys her widower father and does not compromise when taken on a stargazing date that involves one blanket.

Landon tells her father: "Jamie has faith in me. She makes me want to be different . . . better."

The screenplay is not as overtly religious as the book. Nevertheless, reluctant Warner Bros. executives pressed Di Novi for hard evidence that an audience existed for such a clean, pro-faith story. The studio eventually sponsored promotional materials for Christian viewers, including 10,000 youth-pastor packets containing a Bible study about issues in the movie.

Now, Di Novi is predicting the film will hit $50 million in theaters, with a bright future in video. This has obvious implications for other films, if there are quality scripts available with a similar blend of morality and storytelling.

"It was hard getting this movie made. I don't mind saying there was spiritual warfare involved," said Di Novi, who is best known for making films such as "Heathers," "Edward Scissorhands" and "Message in a Bottle," based on another Sparks novel.

"This isn't a blockbuster. But it is a bona fide hit movie. People should sit up and pay attention. I think we have shown that there is an audience for a teen movie that isn't just about sex, drugs and rock 'n' roll. You don't have to be prurient."

Christian critics have not been silent or unanimous in their praise. Some powerful voices have insisted that "A Walk to Remember" is too vague. The film does not include one very dangerous word — *Jesus* — and the rebel never articulates his faith. Di Novi said the movie was screened in advance for secular and religious audiences, and she had no intention of running either crowd out of theaters.

The bottom line is that this is not a "Christian movie" that preaches at viewers. Instead, she said her goal was to produce something more daring — a Hollywood movie that revolves around a Christian character that is compassionate and attractive, as opposed to being a phony, angry, hypocritical, judgmental zealot.

At the same time, the movie makes a subtle comment about modern churches and the young people in their pews. It shows the rebellious Landon sitting in church, and, later, a confrontation with the preacher makes it clear the kid was paying some attention week after week.

"Lots of kids go to church, but you never see that reflected in TV and at the movies," said Di Novi. "And there are all kinds of kids at church: good kids and mixed-up kids. The book says Landon had already been baptized. Sometimes the faith gets through to kids like that, and sometimes it doesn't."

HOLLYWOOD AFTER "THE PASSION"

May 2004

The Rev. Mac Brunson recently took his kids out, and while the movie was forgettable, the pastor of the First Baptist Church of Dallas was hooked by one of the coming attractions.

It was a trailer for the comedy "Raising Helen," in which Kate Hudson plays a hot New York City fashion star whose life changes when she has to raise her sister's three children. Five-hankie chick flicks require hunky love interests, and, lo and behold, this time the blonde falls for a handsome, charming pastor.

"I thought, 'No way Hollywood will get that right,'" said Brunson, senior minister of the 12,000-member Southern Baptist megachurch. "You see a pastor in a movie today, and he's almost always going to be an idiotic, dangerous, neurotic pervert or something."

Brunson aired some of these views when he was interviewed for a People magazine cover story called "Does Hollywood Have Faith?" What happened next was a parable about studio insiders trying to do their homework in pews and pulpits. It's a trend that predates "The Passion of the Christ" but is surging along with Mel Gibson's bank account.

After reading Brunson's remarks, publicists working for Disney called and made the preacher an offer he couldn't refuse. Before long, Brunson was sitting in the Tinseltown multiplex in suburban Dallas, watching an advance screening of "Raising Helen" with 200 church members.

The tough Baptist crowd was pleasantly surprised, said Brunson. Yes, the Lutheran pastor was played by John Corbett of "Sex and the City." Yes, this is the rare pastor who never mentions Jesus, faith, church and the Bible when talking with a woman who has three children in his Christian school. But it's clear that Helen is seeking moral stability, and she ultimately decides to embrace her children, rather than worship her career. And the romance was clean.

"It was just a normal movie, or what people used to call normal," he said. "This pastor is a moral guy. He falls in love. He gets to be natural. He's romantic, and he kisses the girl. . . . At the end, it's clear that he's helped stabilize things and they're becoming a real family.

"So hurrah for Disney, on this movie. They got something right, and we ought to praise them for that. Let's hope and pray that they do it some more."

But bridge-building efforts like this are tricky. While Disney is making progress with one powerful Baptist — remember that the Southern Baptist Convention has been boycotting Disney for seven years — MGM is traveling a rocky road trying to evangelize church groups on behalf of its edgy satire called "Saved!"

An online miniguide for youth leaders says the movie presents "Christian teens who make poor choices, have a crisis of faith, seek answers and ultimately emerge with a genuine faith." Studio executives say it contains a pure Christian message of tolerance and love. Meanwhile, producer Michael Stipe — the androgynous REM lead vocalist — has said it's a high-school vampire movie, "only here the monsters are Jesus-freak teenagers."

The movie's American Eagle Christian Academy has a giant plastic Jesus figure (in running shoes), and born-again gunners practice at the Emmanuel Shooting Range ("An eye for an eye"). One girl has a vision to sleep with her boyfriend to cure his homosexuality. The pseudo-hip Pastor Skip has an affair with a troubled mother (the area's top Christian interior decorator). The villain is a true believer who rules the popular girls ("The Christian Jewels") with an ironclad Bible.

The executives behind "Saved!" simply haven't done the "cross-cultural homework" required to reach religious believers, said Walt Mueller, head of the national Center for Parent/Youth Understanding in Elizabethtown, Pa. While much of the movie's satire is accurate and even constructive, it's the actual theological message that will offend most Christians.

"If you're into a real postmodern, smorgasbord, all-tolerant blend of Christianity and every other conceivable faith in the world, then you're going to love this movie," said Mueller. "What is amazing is that the people marketing this movie don't seem to realize that they are attacking lots of people's beliefs. . . .

"The bottom line is that there are good Christians and then there are bad Christians, and Hollywood gets to decide which is which. We're supposed to buy that?"

NOT A "ROOKIE" FAITH

May 2002

Jim Morris came of age in a West Texas town, which means the locals didn't need to use street addresses to tell where they lived.

All he had to say was that his house was one block from Wood Creek Baptist Church and a vacant lot away from the Camp Bowie Sports Complex. That would cover the essentials, out where nobody talks much about the separation of church and sports.

"The first thing you need to understand about West Texas is that even local video stores have announcement boards out front with messages like, 'Keep Christ in Christmas,'" said Morris, in the first line of "The Rookie," the book about his middle-aged ascent into major-league baseball. "The second thing to understand is that, if Jesus Christ himself were to show up on a Friday night in the fall, he'd have to wangle a seat in the high school stadium and wait until the football game ended before declaring his arrival."

Naturally, a whole lot of praying and Bible reading vanished when Walt Disney Pictures got hold of this story. But the good news for fans of old-fashioned movies is that God wasn't totally written out of the plot when "The Rookie" moved to the big screen. It's hard to drain the faith out of a West Texas tale full of baseball, babies, wedding rings, tears, tough love and nuns appealing to the patron saint of impossible dreams.

Morris was a natural athlete who almost reached the big show as a youngster, before his body broke down. So he got married, settled down, started teaching school and coaching a little baseball.

Then the kids on his ragged high school team made him promise to give professional baseball one more shot, if they won the district championship. The team won district. Morris went to a free-agent tryout and discovered that his blown-out shoulder was serving up 98 mile-per-hour fastballs — light years past what he threw in his prime. With the stunned blessing of his wife and three kids, Morris headed to the minor leagues and then, at age 35, to the big leagues.

Roll out the clichés. No Hollywood ink slinger would dare concoct such a story.

"It was God," said Morris, who is busy as a motivational speaker in both religious and secular settings. "What other explanation could there be for what happened?"

"The Rookie" has already passed $70 million in ticket sales, which means Disney succeeded in creating a feel-good hit for baseball season. But the movie raised eyebrows with its G rating, which is often box-office death with adults.

The key is that "The Rookie" is basically an updated version of one of old Hollywood's most popular products: the inspiring story of a good man who beats the odds and wins big. Moviemakers used to tell this kind of story all the time, and they almost always included a healthy dose of faith and family.

As it turns out, this formula still works — if the story is good enough.

"Quite frankly, faith played a big role in my life, so it would have been impossible to have left that out of the movie," said Morris. But the producers of the movie "didn't draw much attention to the religious side of the story."

They didn't have to. It was shocking enough to watch Hollywood tell a simple story about grown-ups and kids chasing their dreams, while keeping their vows and saying a prayer or two. But those who read the book will wonder, in particular, what happened to its major theme, which is the pitcher's ongoing efforts to fathom "God's mysterious ways" of working through both the agony and the triumph of his life.

Nevertheless, God remains in the details, soaked into the images of family and commitment. Morris said his story makes "no sense whatsoever" without the faith element.

"They just sort of hit it, then back away a little," he said. "I thought that was appropriate, to tell you the truth. They didn't try to jam anything down anybody's throat. You didn't want people sitting in theaters saying, 'What are you trying to do here?' . . . This is a movie. You really can't preach at people."

"THE PASSION" AND THE TALMUD

February 2004

The ancient rabbinic text is clear about the punishment for those who twisted sacred law and misled the people of Israel.

Offenders would be stoned and then hung by their hands from two pieces of wood connected to form a "T." The Talmud once included this example from the Sanhedrin.

"On the eve of Passover they hung Jesus of Nazareth," said the passage, which was censored in the 16th century to evade the wrath of Christians. "The herald went out before him for 40 days saying, 'Jesus goes forth to be stoned, because he has practiced magic, enticed and led astray Israel. Anyone who knows anything in his favor, let him come and declare concerning him.' And they found nothing in his favor."

If armies of Jewish and Christian scholars insist on arguing about Mel Gibson's explosive movie "The Passion of the Christ," it would help if they were candid and started dealing with the hard passages in Jewish texts as well as the Christian Scriptures.

At least, that's what David Klinghoffer thinks.

The Orthodox Jewish writer, whose forthcoming book is entitled "Why the Jews Rejected Jesus," believes these lines from the Talmud are as troubling as any included in the Christian Gospels. They are as disturbing as any image Gibson might include in his controversial epic.

The Talmudic text seems clear. Jesus clashed with Jewish leaders, debating them on the meaning of their laws. They hated him. Many wanted him dead.

It is possible, said Klinghoffer, to interpret these documents as saying that Jesus' fate rested entirely with the Jewish court. The use of language such as "enticed and led astray" indicated that Jesus may have been charged with leading his fellow Jews to worship false gods.

There are more details in this confusing drama. Writing in 12th-century Egypt, the great Jewish sage Maimonides summed up the ancient texts.

"Jesus of Nazareth," he proclaims in his Letter to Yemen, ". . . impelled people to believe that he was a prophet sent by God to clarify perplexities in the Torah, and that he was the Messiah that was predicted by each and every seer. He interpreted the Torah and its precepts in such a fashion as to lead to their total annulment, to the abolition of all its commandments and to the violation of its prohibitions.

"The sages, of blessed memory, having become aware of his plans before his reputation spread among our people, meted out fitting punishment to him."

Is that it? What role did the Romans play?

In terms of historic fact, stressed Klinghoffer, it's almost impossible to find definitive answers for such questions. But the purpose of the Jewish oral traditions that led to the Talmud was to convey religious belief, not necessarily historical facts.

"If you really must ask, 'Who is responsible for the death of Jesus?' then you can only conclude that both the Gospels and the

Talmud agree that the Jewish leaders did not have the power to execute him," he said. "Did they influence the event? The religious texts suggest that they did; the historic texts suggest that they did not. It's hard to know. . . . But if Gibson is an anti-Semite, then to be consistent you would have to say that so was Maimonides."

Obviously, Klinghoffer is not spreading this information in order to fan the flames of hatred. His goal, he said, is to provoke Jewish leaders in cities such as New York and Los Angeles to strive harder to understand the views of traditional Protestants and Catholics. And it's time for liberal Christians to spend as much time talking with Orthodox Jews as with liberal Jews.

It's time for everyone to be more honest, he said.

"I don't see anything that is to be gained for Judaism by going out of our way to antagonize a Mel Gibson or to antagonize as many traditional Christians as we possibly can. I think we have been yelling 'Fire!' in a crowded theater," said Klinghoffer.

"To put it another way, I don't think it's very wise for a few Jewish leaders to try to tell millions of Christians what they are supposed to believe. Would we want some Christians to try to edit our scriptures and to tell us what we should believe?"

BEYOND THE BAPTIST BOYCOTT
August 2004

It was a cheesy ad slogan sure to raise eyebrows during the summer battle for the teen-movie bucks — "Got Passion? Get Saved!"

An acidic take on a Christian high school, "Saved!" was crafted to make evangelicals punch their boycott buttons. It featured clean-queen Mandy Moore as a Bible-throwing harpy from Hades. Macaulay

"Home Alone" Culkin played a hip cynic in a wheelchair who shared cigarettes and sex with the school's lone Jewish girl. Its all-tolerant God offered a flexible moral code.

MGM promoted the film directly to believers who were sure to hate it.

"It seemed like they did everything they could to get a boycott," said Walt Mueller, head of the Center for Parent/Youth Understanding in Elizabethtown, Pa. "They wanted a boycott. They needed a boycott. I am sure they were stunned when they didn't get one."

The film cost $5 million to produce and grossed only $8.8 million, after a quiet sojourn in selected theaters. The bottom line: "Saved!" was an intriguing test case for those pondering the impact of media boycotts. Looking ahead, will Southern Baptist executives balk at saying the words *Disney*, *boycott* and *The Chronicles of Narnia* in the same sentence?

The crucial word-of-mouth buzz never arrived for "Saved!" — perhaps because the conservatives the film set out to bash often turned the other cheek and declined to provide millions of dollars in free publicity.

It helped that the film took so many potshots that it even offended some secular scribes.

Michael O'Sullivan of the Washington Post said the best adjective for "Saved!" was "condescending" and that it was "as preachy as its finger-wagging victims." Glenn Whipp of the Los Angeles Daily News said the movie's creators wanted audiences to "know that it's important to practice tolerance of others — unless, of course, those others are Christians."

Still, the Los Angeles Times did its part to help the studio by seeking condemnation from the usual snarky suspects — Catholic League President William Donahue, op-ed columnist Cal Thomas, Christian Film and Television Commission czar Ted Baehr and the Rev. Jerry Falwell. Apparently Pat Robertson was busy that day.

But no one uttered the "b" word: "boycott." "Saved!" didn't even create a buzz at the annual meeting of the Southern Baptist Convention.

"I vaguely remember hearing of that movie, but that's about it," said Dwayne Hastings of the Ethics and Religious Liberty Commission media office. "I didn't get a single call about it or a single e-mail. It simply did not make a blip on the Southern Baptist radar."

This is interesting, since Hollywood remains a hot issue for Southern Baptists and other moral conservatives. Years after the national headlines, the 1997 Southern Baptist vote to boycott the Walt Disney Co. remains in effect. The convention cited a wave of "anti-Christian" media products, Disney policies granting benefits to partners of gay employees and "Gay Day" events at theme parks that angered many families and church groups.

There is no sign that the Southern Baptist leadership is rethinking this stance. This summer, the Rev. Wiley Drake of First Baptist in Buena Vista, Calif., a strong Disney critic, floated a convention resolution commending the studio for producing the patriotic movie "America's Heart and Soul." His motion was ruled out of order.

"I want a specific action commending them for what they are doing," said Drake.

Hastings said it's hard to image the convention retreating and ending the boycott. It's just as hard to imagine Disney apologizing to Southern Baptists. Nevertheless, an upcoming series of films based on the fantasy fiction of the best-known Christian writer of the 20th century would certainly raise questions. What if Mel Gibson provided the voice of Aslan, the Christ-figure lion?

"It's possible that there could be a resolution praising Disney for doing 'Narnia.' Of course, this assumes that they offer some kind of accurate rendering of the Christian vision and beliefs of C.S. Lewis," said Hastings.

"But the whole point of the boycott is for people to stop and think about their choices. I'm sure that millions of Baptists went to see 'Finding Nemo,' and they watch ESPN like everybody else. But they are thinking twice about giving Disney their money and support. People are learning to be more selective."

GOD ON TV

Christianity was the one great assumption of Christendom.
I can think of no entity today capable of such
a culturally unifying role except television.
In television, we live and move and have our being.
— KENNETH A. MYERS[1]

The book cover was strange, and, frankly, I wasn't interested at all.

It showed a lamb standing meekly near a pool of water, but there was a ferocious lion in the reflection. This pointed toward the generic title, the kind that Christian publishers pin on dozens of volumes each year. It was called "Roaring Lambs: A Gentle Plan to Radically Change Your World." The author was Bob Briner, president of ProServ Television. I vaguely remembered his byline on some newspaper op-ed columns, which turned out to be right. He had been published in The New York Times, The Wall Street Journal and elsewhere.

I didn't have time to read a fuzzy Christian book in the summer of 1993, as I was packing up my Denver Seminary office to move to

Milligan College in the East Tennessee mountains. However, the person who brought me the book was Dr. Vernon Grounds, a quiet but feisty scholar best known as one of the founders of Evangelicals for Social Action. As I write this, he is 91 years old and still working, which means he is adding books to the 23,000-volume personal collection that bears his name in the seminary library.

The man knows books. He handed me "Roaring Lambs" and said, "It may not look like it, but you need to see this."

The back cover of the book was, in its own way, stranger than the front. It contained blurbs from Bill Moyers of PBS, tennis legend Arthur Ashe, "Terms of Endearment" producer Martin Jurow, author and preacher Ray Pritchard, major-league baseball star Dave Dravecky and philosopher D. Elton Trueblood. The final endorsement was from Newsweek star Frank Deford, who wrote: "Too often the message of Christianity today is promulgated by 'professional' Christians, smugly preaching to the converted. More difficult and more noteworthy — even more Christian — is what Bob Briner advocates, that what matters is to carry the Word and its goodness into the skeptical, multicultural, real world."

What in the world? I thought. Who is this guy?

Within a few paragraphs, I hit a broadside in which Briner called the modern church "almost a nonentity when it comes to shaping culture. . . . [The] church has abdicated its role as salt and light." Then I read this: "My point is really quite simple. Look around you. Can you honestly say that Christian influence is felt in Hollywood? . . . That when you turn on the television you are aware of an underlying foundation of Judeo-Christian values in that medium?"[2]

The next day, my telephone rang. It was an advance person for Briner, saying that he was coming to Denver to do some work related to his many cable-television projects. Briner had read some of my columns and wanted to meet me to discuss the ideas in his book. Would I like to meet him?

The massive former basketball player and football coach showed up a few days later and helped me pack. Then he sat down on a heavy box, and we talked about his three decades of wrestling with issues of faith and mass media, with an emphasis on why religious believers have so much trouble doing quality television.

Briner started in a strange place, asking if I had seen emotional church services in which preachers plead with the faithful to commit their lives to foreign missions. They end with young people kneeling at the altar, while parents shed brave tears. Maybe it's time, he said, to hold a different kind of church service — challenging young people to enter another hostile culture. Take network television, for example.

"Sure, I know that there are spiritual risks involved in the media," he said. "But most Christians don't want to get involved in the hard work of providing any alternatives, when it comes to TV, movies, art, music or the news media. . . . It's so much easier just to be self-righteous and to complain, rather than to put the time and the money and the energy into realistic efforts to help shape our culture. It's easier to complain and to whine. Then, when media people bash us, we can complain and whine about that, too."

Christians seem determined to make niche TV programs for other believers, he said. They don't seem to realize that the greatest challenge — even when wielding the awesome power of mainstream television — is changing the minds of those who do not believe what you believe. It's easy to impress those who are already on your side. What is hard is creating dozens and dozens of solid, commercial, even innovative television programs that appeal to people who are still trying to make up their minds. It is even harder to find winsome, witty ways to soften the rock-hard beliefs of those who clearly are your enemies, in terms of public debates.

No, most Christians would rather just "preach to the choir," he said, a natural metaphor for a man who, in those days, lived in

Dallas. Most Christians would rather just use television to fire up their troops and raise money.

It was the start of a long conversation, which only ended when cancer ended Briner's life in 1999. But he left a legacy in his media work and in the lives of the young believers he touched.

When I think of Briner, which is often, I remember that he was haunted by two quotes from philosopher D. Elton Trueblood. One says that it is "hard to exaggerate the degree to which the modern church seems irrelevant to modern man," and the other adds that the "test of the vitality of a religion is to be seen in its effect upon culture."

Keep that in mind when reading TV Guide.

BEYOND "BECKY GOES TO BIBLE CAMP"
May 1999

GREENVILLE, Ill. — After 35 years of work in television and sports, Bob Briner is a pro at spotting doors of opportunity in the numbers churned out by media-research firms.

So he wasn't surprised that the new Internet-based Digital Entertainment Network is poised to webcast a show called "Redemption High." This post-MTV drama will, according to USA Today, center on "several Christian teens, a group almost completely ignored by broadcast television. . . . The teens grapple with problems by asking themselves what Jesus would do in their situation."

The twist isn't who is producing "Redemption High," but who is not.

"It's stunning that the people at a hip outfit like DEN would see this opening right there in the demographics," said Briner, co-founder and president of ProServ Television in Dallas and a global pioneer in pro tennis and other sports media. "But of course they saw it! It should be obvious this audience is waiting out there. . . . What's so amazing and so sad is that Christian people still can't see it."

The former basketball player and football coach laughed and waved his giant hand, like he was backhanding a pesky gnat. "Let's face it: Most Christians still won't get behind a project in the entertainment business unless you're gonna make 'Becky Goes to Bible Camp,'" he said.

Briner is a conservative churchman, and he doesn't enjoy making this kind of wisecrack. Nevertheless, the 63-year-old entrepreneur has — beginning with a 1993 book called "Roaring Lambs" — grown increasingly candid in his critiques of the religious establishment. His work has had an especially strong impact in Nashville, the Bible Belt's entertainment capital.

Now, after writing or co-writing seven books in six years, Briner is working with even greater urgency. The early title for his next book is "Christians Have Failed America: And Some of Us Are Sorry." He is writing it while fighting cancer.

Most Christians, he argues in the first chapter, are sinfully content to write for other Christians, sing to other Christians, produce television programs for other Christians, educate other Christians, debate other Christians and only do business with other Christians.

"Shameful," he writes. "We have failed and are failing America. I am sorry. In failing to show up . . . in the places that really count, where the moral, ethical and spiritual health of our country is concerned, we have left our country exposed and vulnerable to all the ills we now see besetting it. We have not provided a way of escape, even though we profess to know the way."

It's a sobering message. But the key is that Briner is both successful — an Emmy winner who has worked with Arthur Ashe, Dave Dravecky, Michael Jordan and many others — and the kind of generous mentor who has voluntarily helped scores of rookies. A few years ago, he sold his homes in Dallas and Paris and moved to central Illinois to work in a one-stoplight town with students at his alma mater, Greenville College.

"Bob is a gadfly — but one with tremendous grace — who prods the church along and asks that we take risks, practice excellence and humbly direct praise to God," said Dave Palmer, an executive at Squint Entertainment in Nashville. Briner, he said, keeps stressing that work must be "recognized on its artistic merits first and not ghetto-ized by any confining terms."

Still, most believers find it easier to blame the secular media for all of society's ills, rather than doing the hard work of funding and creating quality alternatives.

"Basically, we continue to take the easy way out," said Briner. "You can't offer the gospel to people if you aren't there in the marketplace and if you have never earned the right to even talk to them. We have failed to give people the chance to choose good things instead of bad things. We have not offered them the best that we have. . . .

"Producing a 'Chariots of Fire' every 25 years or so won't get it done. We have to produce a 'Chariots of Fire' every week or every day if we are serious about giving people an alternative worldview to what Hollywood is selling them."

GOD, MAN AND "THE SIMPSONS"
November 2000

The King James Version of the Bible is a masterpiece of the English language and one of the cornerstones of Western Civilization as we know it.

So sociologist John Heeren perked up when he was watching

"The Simpsons" and heard a reference to a "St. James Version." Was this a nod to an obscure translation? An inside-baseball joke about fundamentalists who confuse the King James of 1611 with the ancient St. James?

Eventually he decided it was merely a mistake, a clue that the writers of that particular script didn't excel in Sunday school. But with "The Simpsons," you never know.

"You only have to watch a few episodes to learn that there's far more religious content in 'The Simpsons' than other shows, especially other comedies," said Heeren, who teaches at California State University, San Bernardino. And the masterminds behind Homer, Marge, Bart, Lisa and Maggie are not doing "a slash-and-burn job, while working in as much blasphemy as possible. . . . They show a surprising respect for the role that religion plays in American life."

Eventually, Heeren became so intrigued that he analyzed 71 episodes of the animated series, taping reruns at random. Now in its 12th season, "The Simpsons" just aired its 250th episode. This milestone came shortly after Heeren presented his findings before the Society for the Scientific Study of Religion. He found that 69 percent of the episodes contained at least one religious reference, and, in 11 percent, the plot centered on a religious issue.

But the hot question is whether the show's take on religion is "good" or "bad." Of course, the whole point of "The Simpsons" is to satirize American life — from TV to public education, from politics to fast food, from rock 'n' roll to religion. Faith is just part of the mix.

But this is where things get complicated, said Heeren. The show specializes in mocking the generic pseudo-religion found in American popular culture.

"It's really about the religion that we see through the filter of the movies and television," he said. "So we are dealing with a copy of a copy. . . . This only raises a bigger question. When you have a satire of a satire, does that mean that you are actually being positive?"

Several religious themes appear over and over, said Heeren. One is that God has a plan — even for Homer and Bart. This concept appears so often that it cannot simply be dismissed as a joke. It also is clear that God is omnipresent and, to one degree or another, omnipotent.

In the "Homer the Heretic" episode, do-gooder daughter Lisa proclaims that a fire in the family's house is evidence that God wants Homer to return to church, instead of practicing a do-it-yourself faith called "Homerism." Heeren notes: "Homer wonders why a fire that began at his house spread to the house of his devout neighbor, Ned Flanders, or 'Charley Church.' . . . Homer asks why God didn't save Flanders' house. At that moment a cloud appears above the Flanders house, puts out the fire, and is punctuated by a rainbow."

The show's writers also consistently contrast two symbolic characters, said the sociologist. On one side is Pastor Timothy Lovejoy, an often cynical, world-weary mainline shepherd who uses the public library's Bible and says that the world's religions are "all pretty much the same." On the other side is Flanders, a born-again nerd who, nevertheless, is one of the only inspiring characters in the series.

Lovejoy, Homer and many other characters appear to be making up their religious beliefs as they go along, said Heeren. But Flanders is a true believer. What is fascinating is that the other characters often "see the light" and eventually try to act a little more like Flanders. As a result, "The Simpsons" almost always ends up affirming some element of a generic Judeo-Christian American creed — honesty, family, community, selflessness and love.

"I'm not sure what that says, but it says something," said Heeren. "What remains is that strange kind of respect that is so hard to pin down. . . . God is real. God hears prayers, and prayers are answered. People go to church. Faith matters. Let's face it: This is not what you normally see in prime-time television."

FREUD MEETS LEWIS ON PBS
September 2004

Dr. Armand Nicholi of Harvard Medical School was caught off guard as he read evaluations of his first seminar on the life and philosophy of Sigmund Freud, the father of psychoanalysis.

"Several of the students said the same thing," he said, recalling that semester 35 years ago. They thought the class "was good, but that it was totally unbalanced. They said it was one sustained attack on the spiritual world."

Nicholi had a problem. He decided that the students were right, but he knew it would be hard to find another writer with the stature to stand opposite Freud — perhaps the 20th century's most influential intellectual. Then he remembered a small book he discovered by chance during his internship in a New York City hospital, a time when he wrestled with the agonizing questions of cancer patients and their loved ones.

The book was "The Problem of Pain" by C.S. Lewis, the Oxford don and Christian apologist. Nicholi revamped his seminar, focusing it on the life stories and writings of Freud and Lewis. Rather than back into discussions of spiritual questions, the psychiatrist placed them at the heart of the syllabus. Decades later, Nicholi's classic course became "The Question of God," a book that has inspired a pair of PBS and Walden Media documentaries for television and home video.

The format blends academics and drama. Nicholi presents Freud as a spokesman for a "secular worldview" that denies the existence of any truth or reality outside the material world. Lewis is the champion of a "spiritual worldview" that accepts the reality of God. Seven articulate women and men representing a variety of viewpoints join in the seminar discussions.

Freud and Lewis are represented by their own words, the commentary of experts and actors who dramatize a few episodes from their lives, often seen in counterpoint with archival photographs and film footage.

Nicholi said the goal is the same as in the seminar — to let these giants grapple with the big questions of life: Is there a God? What is happiness? Why do people suffer? Is death the end? What is the source for morality? It helps that Lewis, before his conversion, was an articulate atheist and familiar with Freud's work.

"I was astonished at how Freud would raise a question and then Lewis would attempt to answer it," said Nicholi. "When you read their work, it is almost as if they are standing side by side at podiums, debating one another. It was uncanny."

At the center of the project is a word that is criticized by some scholars: "worldview." Nicholi said it's impossible to deny that Lewis and Freud had different approaches to life. Each saw the world through filters created by culture, heritage, philosophy, education, experiences, faith and prejudices.

Their actions and writings make no sense when separated from these secular and sacred worldviews, said Nicholi. By studying their worldviews, students can test and refine their own. Many educators seem afraid to even discuss this process, he said. They find it especially hard to discuss questions of faith and morality.

"You can study an opposing worldview and learn everything that you can about it, or you can try to ignore it," said Nicholi. "Many religious believers are afraid to take Freud's work seriously. They reject him out of hand. On the other side are the critics of Lewis who say that his traditional Christian beliefs were fitting for the uneducated masses, but not for the classroom. You hear them say, 'I do not consider this is an intelligent point of view and, since I am intelligent, I don't have to pay attention to it.'"

This is education?

Through the years, Nicholi has defended his seminar from critics on both sides. He still finds it hard to believe that people who claim to cherish academic freedom and diversity can question the value of reading and contrasting the works of these two intellectual heavyweights.

"We are supposed to be as critical, as objective and as dispassionate as we can possibly be," said Nicholi. "But if we cannot allow this kind of dialogue between two worldviews to take place in an academic setting, then we are in trouble. Discussing these kinds of questions is what academic life is supposed to be about."

THE VERY
REV. TED TURNER SPEAKS
March 2001

Once again, the Very Rev. Ted Turner has bravely stepped forward to blaze new trails for peace, love and religious tolerance.

And all the people said, "Say what?"

"I was looking at this woman and I was trying to figure out what was on her forehead," said the founder of the Cable News Network, during a retirement party for anchorman Bernard Shaw. Looking around, Turner realized it was Ash Wednesday and several other Catholics were standing nearby.

"What are you, a bunch of Jesus freaks?" he asked. "You ought to be working for Fox."

There was nothing particularly shocking about the latest statement from the vice chairman of AOL Time Warner Inc. After all, the Mouth of the South has previously said that Christianity is "for losers," pro-lifers are bozos and the pope is a Polish idiot. Perhaps he was shocked to see signs of Lenten repentance in his newsroom and was caught off guard.

But the key to this story came when Turner responded to the latest howls of outrage from his critics.

"I apologize to all Christians for my comment about Catholics wearing ashes on their foreheads," he said. "I do not believe in any form of prejudice or discrimination, especially religious intolerance."

If his sermons are to be taken seriously, Turner is openly campaigning for the role of religious leader and prophet. By holding himself up as an advocate of religious tolerance, he also is implying that his enemies are the true advocates of religious intolerance.

Turner spoke at length on this topic in a highly confessional address to more than 1,000 rabbis, swamis, monks, ministers and other spiritual leaders at the United Nations. Of course, the media leader did more than speak at the Millennium World Peace Summit of Religious and Spiritual Leaders — he helped create it.

As a boy, stressed Turner, he had wanted to be a Christian missionary. But now, he said, he understands that missionaries are the enemies of truth and tolerance.

"Instead of all these different gods," he said, "maybe there's one God who manifests himself and reveals himself in different ways to different people. How about that? . . . Basically, the major religions which have survived today don't have blood sacrifice, and they don't have hatred behind them. Those which have done the best are the ones that are built on love."

Thus, he concluded: "It's time to get rid of hatred. It's time to get rid of prejudice. It's time to have love and respect and tolerance for each other."

Turner doesn't consider himself anti-religious. He is merely opposed to religious groups that he believes are intolerant of other faith groups. Turner believes he is not anti-Christian. He is opposed to Christians who still believe that Jesus is the only path to salvation.

And Turner is not anti-Catholic, per se. He financially supports Catholics who oppose their church's teachings on messy, personal subjects such as sex and salvation.

And Turner is not alone in seeing direct links between missionaries and hate groups, between evangelism and violence.

As part of a global United Religions Initiative, California Episcopal bishop William Swing has said that in order for "religions to pursue peace among each other, there will have to be a godly cease-fire, a temporary truce where the absolute, exclusive claims of each will be honored, but an agreed-upon neutrality will be exercised in terms of proselytizing, condemning, murdering or dominating. These will not be tolerated in the United Religions zone."

Critics who think Turner and his allies are anti-religious crusaders are not seeing the big picture, said Mary Jo Anderson, a contributing editor at the Catholic journal Crisis. There's a reason Turner is so critical of religious groups that he believes are mired in the past. He is convinced that he is helping create the religion of the future.

"Ted Turner has a kind of vision," she said. "He sees a world in which everyone is free to live the way Western man lives, with three TVs, two BMWs and one child. He believes man is evolving spiritually, as well as physically. . . . He is absolutely sure that he is going to be a leader in what happens next."

OPRAH, "BABE" AND RELIGIOUS LIBERTY

March 1996

It's hard to debate religious liberty issues with a superstar pig from Hollywood.

The star of "Babe, the Gallant Pig" made a cameo appearance during the taping of an Oprah Winfrey show about Bible readings and prayers in public schools in Pontotoc, Miss. The talking pig — on video — interrupted the host's opening narration about "people who have been made to feel like outcasts in their own communities."

While plugging the movie, "Babe" stressed its timely message: the importance of loving one another and having an "unprejudiced heart." Sure enough, this sound bite later fit perfectly in yet another television drama about the Religious Right. . . .

"There's really not much you can do," said Michael Whitehead, a Southern Baptist attorney representing the school district. "You can either play their game and look like a cad or be silent and not defend yourself. . . . If you choose to take them on, then it's really hard not to appear angry. After all, the whole game is set up to produce fireworks."

In this case, the local school board allowed student-led prayers and Bible readings, resulting in a lawsuit by the American Civil Liberties Union and People for the American Way. In addition to attorneys, the "Oprah" show featured citizens who back the school board as well as those who contacted the ACLU, Lisa Herdahl and her son, Kevin.

Beforehand, Whitehead said that Winfrey's staff seemed surprised that many in the studio audience supported voluntary prayer. Thus, they hunted for those willing to take the other side in a "spontaneous" debate.

Producers have to find out who will do the best job of stating strong opinions on the air, said Jill Almquist, an "Oprah" publicist. Also, it's customary to move these people to designated chairs, to help the camera crews. "We do ask, 'Who can we go to?'. . . But we don't like people to do too much talking . . . because we want to save the excitement for the show itself," she said.

From Whitehead's perspective, it appeared that the producer, after generating "passionate and heated exchanges," then set out to tape a show about "how awful it is that people in Pontotoc have . . . strong, passionate convictions." Also, Winfrey's script suggested that Christian activists engaged in, or condoned, alleged death threats and harassment.

"People are seeing images of students praying around a flagpole or holding a rally," said Whitehead. "But Oprah's doing a voice-over that says something like, 'How would it feel to get up in the morning not knowing if this day would be your last or to wonder if you'll be shot on the way to the supermarket?'"

Ironically, recent research — including work by conservatives — indicates that "Oprah" is now one of talk TV's least sensationalistic shows. Also, Winfrey openly embraces religion. While her beliefs may be unorthodox, and her personal life is tabloid territory, she often goes out of her way to use language such as "the God that I love loves all of us, no matter what" or to say that she is a practicing Christian.

"The studio audience always ends up applauding as Oprah defends Christianity," said Whitehead, who was making his second appearance on Winfrey's show. "She's the champion of a loving Christianity, and, obviously, anyone who takes a different approach represents a mean, judgmental Christianity."

The result is a powerful form of television that addresses serious public issues, while emphasizing entertainment, opinion and, above all, visual images. While it's hard to know what editors will choose as a finale for this show, Whitehead predicted it will be an emotional statement by Kevin Herdahl, followed by Winfrey's reprise of the gospel according to "Babe."

"It's a classic. You have a teenager saying, 'Can't we all just get along?' with tears running down his cheeks," he said. "You can't argue with a teenager's tears. So much for student-initiated, student-led prayers and Bible studies. So much for a fair debate. . . . It all comes down to tears and a Hollywood pig."

JIM BAKKER'S OTHER CONSPIRACY

December 1996

It's impossible to tell Jim Bakker's story without mentioning his conspiracy theories.

The former PTL leader has always felt that people were conspiring against him — especially journalists, politicians and judges. After the 1987 collapse of his empire, he said he had been betrayed by other televangelists.

Naturally, Bakker adds variations on these themes in his tell-all memoir, "I Was Wrong." But one of its most intriguing details is evidence of yet another conspiracy that he doesn't want to discuss. Note this angry passage in Bakker's remarks as he resigned as PTL's president.

"I sorrowfully acknowledge that seven years ago . . . I was wickedly manipulated by treacherous former friends and colleagues who victimized me with the aid of a female confederate," he said. "They conspired to betray me into a sexual encounter at a time of great stress in my marital life. . . . I was set up as part of a scheme to co-opt me and obtain some advantage for themselves over me in connection with their hope for position in the ministry."

In other words, the first domino at PTL was a scheme that preceded Bakker's 1980 sexual liaison with Jessica Hahn, a conspiracy within his inner circle that preceded "Pearlygate."

Yet Bakker has nothing new to say about these "friends and colleagues" and their scheme. In particular, he downplays the role of the bisexual evangelist John Wesley Fletcher, who arranged the tryst with Hahn, and he hardly mentions James and David Taggart, the brothers who many claim controlled Bakker in his final PTL years.

In his book, Bakker confesses many sins. He repents of his "health and wealth" theology, saying he sinfully twisted Scripture. He offers 647 pages of near-stream-of-consciousness details about lessons he learned during his trial, divorce and prison years. But he continues to avoid some questions.

"For most Pentecostal and charismatic people, the most serious questions about Jim Bakker were all those allegations of moral misconduct. . . . People haven't forgotten that," said historian Vinson Synan of Regent University in Virginia Beach, Va. "There does appear to have been a kind of subterranean, homosexual world inside PTL that has never been fully described. That's where so many questions remain."

Many of the questions center on Fletcher. In addition to his ties to Hahn, it was Fletcher who made anonymous calls in 1983 spreading dirt about Bakker. Several of those calls went to me, when I was working as a religion writer in Charlotte, N.C., and I later shared my information with reporter Charles E. Shepard, author of "Forgiven: The Rise and Fall of Jim Bakker and the PTL Ministry." Years later, Shepard confirmed that Fletcher was my mystery caller.

Fletcher mentioned Hahn by name in 1983 and also said David Taggart was Bakker's lover. Fletcher was bitter and said Bakker had failed to keep promises and had forsaken him during tough times. But Fletcher did not, during those calls, say what he later said during the "Pearlygate" media storm — that he, too, had been sexually involved with Bakker.

"I never knew a more corrupt person in my life, period, than Jim Bakker," Fletcher told me. "Now I see him for what he is."

Today, those at the Massapequa (N.Y.) Full Gospel Tabernacle Church, where Fletcher preached in the early '90s, refuse to answer questions, merely saying that he recently passed away. Tabloid reports said he suffered from AIDS.

The key: Did Fletcher try to manipulate Bakker to gain power at PTL, starting a chain reaction? Or did Bakker betray Fletcher?

"I Was Wrong" neither asks nor answers this question. On the homosexuality issue, Bakker does include a chapter saying that, as a teen, he was molested — for several years — by a young man he knew at church. This left Bakker confused about his own sexual identity and he said that while in prison he sought, and received, assurances from a counselor that he isn't gay.

And so the story continues, with Bakker attempting a comeback as a humbled counselor for those who face pain in their own lives. Yet he clearly knows that his return is threatened more by the ghosts of his complicated sexual past than by the legal demons that sent him to prison.

CARL SAGAN: TELEVANGELIST

January 1997

While he often played the role of scientific high priest, the late Carl Sagan didn't own a set of liturgical vestments.

Thus, he wore his academic regalia as he ascended into the pulpit of New York's Cathedral of St. John the Divine on Oct. 3, 1993, the Feast of St. Francis. The rite for the day — the "Missa Gaia (Earth Mass)" — included taped cries of wolves and whales and a procession featuring an elephant, a camel, a vulture, a swarm of bees and a bowl of blue-green algae. Musicians sang praises to Ra, Ausar and other gods, as well as to Jehovah.

The astronomer was right at home, weaving threads of science into a mystical litany — while remaining light years from theism.

"Life fills every nook and cranny of our planet's surface," said Sagan. "There are bacteria in the upper air, jumping spiders at the tops of the highest mountains, sulfur-metabolizing worms in the deep ocean trenches and heat-loving microbes kilometers below the surface of the land. Almost all of these beings are in intimate contact. They eat and drink one another, breathe each other's waste gases, inhabit one another's bodies. . . . They have generated a web of mutual dependence and interaction that embraces the planet."

After his death on Dec. 20, Sagan was praised for his work as director of Cornell University's Laboratory for Planetary Studies, as a Pulitzer Prize-winning author and as an apologist for science on public television. He was the rare intellectual who could trade gags with Johnny Carson.

Truth is, Sagan was a talented "TV evangelist," said Robert C. Newman, who, while he has a Cornell doctorate in astrophysics, teaches at Biblical Theological Seminary in Hatfield, Pa. Sagan even opened his most famous programs with an unbeliever's creed: "The Cosmos is all that is or ever was or ever will be."

"Now, by Sagan's own definition of the methodology of science, this is not a scientific statement. This is a religious statement," said Newman, in a 1981 lecture at Cornell. Sagan could not have researched everything in the past, and it's impossible to do lab work in the future. Thus, "the Cosmos is all that is" must be considered a "faith statement," said Newman.

After the Mass at St. John the Divine, I asked Sagan whether his religious views had evolved in recent years. Was he, perhaps, trying to create a kind of modern deism or some fusion of science and Eastern spirituality?

Sagan said that while some of his images may have changed, he continued to reject the notion of a transcendent God that exists outside the world, universe or cosmos.

"I remain inexorably opposed to any kind of revealed religion and reject any talk of a personal god," said Sagan, while posing for news crews with clergy on the cathedral steps. "But millions of people believe in a god that is not that kind of god." Using the classic image of a divine watchmaker, he added: "Some might say, for example, that there is some kind of force or power in the watch — a set of laws, perhaps. Then the watch creates itself. I'm more comfortable with that kind of language."

In his novel, "Contact," Sagan was very specific about which religions can embrace this concept and which cannot. In a debate with a Christian, his protagonist explains why she rejects belief in the God of Judaism, Christianity and Islam.

"When I say I'm an agnostic, I only mean that the evidence isn't in," says astronomer Eleanor Arroway, played by actress Jodie Foster in the Hollywood movie. "There isn't compelling evidence that God exists — at least your kind of god — and there isn't compelling evidence that he doesn't." By the end of the book, Sagan's heroine accepts that the universe was "made on purpose" and contains evidence of an "artist's signature."

At that point, said Newman, Sagan may have been "dabbling with the concept of a god. . . . He may even have been moving toward some form of pantheism. It's hard to tell. What we do know is that he remained totally opposed to the God of the Bible."

VEGGIES ATTACK THE FUNNY GAP

October 2002

While flipping through TV channels the other night, VeggieTales writer Mike Nawrocki discovered an absolutely hilarious preacher.

We're not talking about the big hair, molasses and glitz humor that makes so many televangelists laugh-to-keep-from-crying funny. No, this preacher was using humor to communicate. He knew his people, and he knew how to make them laugh.

"It was very, very funny. But he was doing this in his own pulpit for his own people," said Nawrocki, who is "Larry the Cucumber" for 25 million VeggieTales video buyers. "I don't know if this preacher would have felt free to be that funny anywhere else. I don't know if he could have been funny outside his church."

Making ordinary people laugh is serious business to Nawrocki and his colleagues at Big Idea Productions, an independent company built on the silly idea of vegetables acting out Bible stories. The twist in this tale is that the VeggieTales people have created a brand of humor that sells in mainstream superstores as well as in small Christian outlets. They don't just joke with the choir.

Now Larry the Cucumber, Bob the Tomato, Junior Asparagus and the virtual vegetables have jumped to the big screen, where they face the long knives of secular critics and consumers. "Jonah: A VeggieTales Movie" opens in 1,100 theaters nationwide. Once again, the Big Idea team is chasing kids 8 years old and younger, while wooing parents with jokes based on Monty Python, "Jaws," "Lawrence of Arabia," "The Blues Brothers" and pop culture.

Industry experts are watching to see if the VeggieTales are truly funny — not church sanctuary funny, but suburban multiplex funny.

"We all know that Christians have trouble with humor," said Nawrocki. "Part of the problem is that all humor is irreverent, in one way or another. But the biggest problem Christians have with comedy is that they're afraid of offending other Christians. So much of humor is rooted in hard truths, and Christians are not fond of hard truths, especially if they're about the church itself."

Nawrocki and Phil "Bob the Tomato" Vischer have wrestled with these issues ever since they were tossed out of Bible college in the mid-1980s. Soon, they were combining their puppetry and comedy skills with computer animation and dreaming about taking on Mickey Mouse.

Meanwhile, they watched their hip friends turn into pastors and youth ministers.

"The implicit message I received growing up was that full-time ministry was the only valid Christian service," said Vischer, founder of Big Idea. "Young Christians were to aspire to be either ministers or missionaries. . . . But I wanted to make movies. And from the movies and TV shows I watched growing up and the influence they had on me, I figured God could use a filmmaker or two, regardless of what anyone else said."

The key, said Vischer, is that he was raised in a culture in which everybody went to church. Then he ventured into the harsh world of advertising and corporate media, and he had to reach people who never went to church. When he created Big Idea, Vischer was determined to create humor that blended both cultures.

Vischer and Nawrocki wanted to make videos, and now movies, that are openly religious, but not aimed at pews. They did not, in other words, want to settle for making "Christian movies." As another Christian in the entertainment industry, David McFadzean of the sitcom "Home Improvement," once quipped, the typical "Christian movie" is very similar to a porno movie. "It has terrible acting. It has a tiny budget. And you know exactly how it's going to end."

That quote is funny yet painfully true, said Vischer.

"We seem to think every artistic expression by a Christian artist, to be valid, must end with an 'altar call.' It's the equivalent of saying every valid football play must end in the end zone," he said. Thus, "many of our efforts are so philosophically aggressive that they read more like war propaganda than entertainment, effectively limiting our audience to only the most committed faithful.

"The end result is that our work and our worldview have little or no impact on the broader culture. We've effectively taken ourselves out of the game."

HOME-SCHOOLERS: THE ANTI-WOODSTOCK GENERATION
September 1999

It seemed like a good idea at the time.

Why not produce, thought conservative activist Paul Weyrich, a library of educational videotapes to help home-school parents? Perhaps even a cable-television channel that offered quality classroom materials mixed with a little wholesome entertainment?

"It made sense to me," said Weyrich, a veteran media entrepreneur and one of the founding fathers of the Religious Right. "But the idea didn't get very far. I've been asking home-schoolers about this for several years, and a lot of them keep telling me, 'We don't have cable. We don't even have a TV.' Many of them are unplugged — literally."

These are not business-as-usual families, cookie-cut into the sizes and shapes on display in shopping malls, mail-order catalogs and, especially, prime-time television. They have unique priorities when they budget their time and money. They have radically different family values that often defy simple political labels.

In a strange way, home-schoolers are creating a new counterculture outside the American mainstream: the Anti-Woodstock Generation.

No one has showered more praise on this crowd than Weyrich. He is ecstatic that 1.5 million or so children are now being educated at home, a number that will only rise in the wake of school-day disasters such as the bloodshed in Littleton, Colo. Even mainstream politicians are starting to pay attention, as symbolized by the GOP presidential hopefuls who paraded through a Home School Legal Defense Association convention in Washington, D.C.

"You have shamed the regular school system with what you have achieved," said billionaire Steve Forbes.

In Texas, Gov. George W. Bush said reverently, "We view home schooling as something to be respected and something to be protected. Respected for the energy and the commitment of loving mothers and loving fathers. Protected from the interference of government."

But Weyrich went much further, in a speech sandwiched between the flashbulb festivals that greeted the heavyweights. If there is hope for this culture, Weyrich told the faithful, "it's because of what you people are doing. Now what we need to do is replicate what you're doing in a whole number of other areas of American life."

Last February, Weyrich made precisely the same point in a controversial letter in which he said moral conservatives have won some political victories but have done little to cleanse the "ever-wider sewer" of American popular culture.

"Politics has failed because of the collapse of the culture. What Americans would have found absolutely intolerable only a few years ago, a majority now not only tolerates but celebrates," he said. "Americans have adopted, in large measure, the MTV culture that we so valiantly opposed just a few years ago, and it has permeated the thinking of all but those who have separated themselves from the contemporary culture."

The Weyrich letter made waves for obvious reasons. Here was the man who coined the phrase "moral majority," now saying that the moral majority was gone. The founder of the Heritage Foundation was saying that America's cultural heritage was in ruins. The president of the Free Congress Foundation was saying that the GOP-driven Congress had sold out on moral issues.

Meanwhile, home-school families were getting the job done, he said. They stopped spinning their wheels in existing educational systems and did something positive. Weyrich believes that the same thing needs to happen in entertainment, journalism, politics, higher education and even in many American religious groups.

But there's one problem. Remember all those unplugged TVs?

It will be hard for home-schooled children to have any cultural impact, said Weyrich, if they've been systematically taught to reject all of their culture — the good as well as the bad. This hit home when he tried to find talented Christian humorists to take part in an alternative television project.

"If we totally drop out, we aren't going to produce any alternative voices in American life," said Weyrich. "We won't have any humor or music or movies or literature or anything else that Americans will be able to turn to, when the culture hits bottom. We really can't afford to become the new Amish. That would be a disaster for us and, I believe, for America."

VANILLA VALUES ON THE D.C. MALL

September 2003

The program opened with a homily by President Bush about American values, teamwork, dedication and the National Football League.

It ended with Aretha Franklin singing the national anthem, with the glare of red rockets reaching the dome of the U.S. Capitol.

Washington Redskins great Joe Theismann reverently called it "a national moment of remembrance," saluting thousands of uniformed military personnel in the crowd. ABC Sports and "New Pepsi Vanilla and Diet Pepsi Vanilla, the Not-So-Vanilla Vanilla" simply called it NFL Kickoff Live 2003.

This prepackaged spectacle on the National Mall was business as usual for most American viewers. But it may have taught a lesson to the 7,000-plus pastors, parents and youth ministers who read and passed on one of Walt Mueller's e-mail alerts to punch "record" on their VCRs and use this as a religious education lab.

"This kind of stuff has become so mainstream that we don't even blink," said Mueller, founder of the Center for Parent/Youth Understanding (www.cpyu.org) in Elizabethtown, Pa. "The whole thing is about mass marketing, of course, but those messages are mixed in there with patriotism, sex, entertainment, sports and everything else. . . .

"This was a peek into the American soul. It said, 'This is what we value. This is what we think is acceptable, good and, of course, cool.'"

The show had something for everyone, from the generic rage of tattooed suburban rockers to bluesy power chords by graying superstars who are eligible for the AARP. Football legends hugged military heroes, while TV producers wrapped everything in red, white and blue.

But the reason many tuned in was to see what former Mickey Mouse Club boy toy Britney Spears would do to top her girl-on-girl love fest with Madonna on the MTV Video Music Awards. The one-time Southern Baptist babe gave it her best shot, lip-syncing her way through gender-bending "freak dance" moves that mimicked sex with reed-thin female dancers as well as the hunky males.

Washington Post critic Tom Shales was amused, in a tired sort of way: "When they weren't being groped or fondled by her, dancers helped Spears strip her pants off, revealing a bikini-like black bottom. . . . They even helped straighten out the little pixie's shorty shorts so that they didn't reveal too much. Or maybe so that they did."

It was a pathetic sight, said Mueller, and many viewers probably laughed. But it's important for adults to see this through the eyes of millions of girls who started watching Spears — with parental blessings — when they were nine or 10 years of age. Now they are entering a time of tremendous physical, emotional and spiritual changes.

What did they see on their television screens?

"Twelve- to 14-year-old girls are not going to watch something like this and say, 'Oh, what a cynical attempt to be shocking in the name of commercialism,'" said Mueller. "No, the girls who grew up with Britney — whether they want to admit it or not — have to see this and think: 'This is how Britney looks now. This is how she acts now. What am I supposed to look like? How am I supposed to behave sexually? This is normal?'"

The goal of the center's "VCR alerts" and similar projects, he said, is to urge adults to pay close attention to how entertainment media provide "maps and mirrors" for young people. When faced with the latest offerings from MTV or the broadcast networks, parents must ask: Why is this happening? How is it affecting our children? How are we supposed to respond?

Instead of carefully thinking through these issues, most adults automatically resort to outrage. Then most sadly realize that they lack the courage or stamina to enforce any media rules in their own homes, especially inside the closed doors of their children's bedrooms.

After a moment of red-faced confrontation, life returns to what is now considered normal. This will not do, said Mueller.

"You have to have your ear to the ground. You have to pay attention," he said. "You have to do this for your kids. You have to do this for the young people at your church. You have to do this because what goes on in their lives really matters."

INK, PAPER AND GOD

The elderly man wore an impeccable gray wool suit and was walking slowly as he carried his CBA shopping bags full of books.

He looked strangely familiar, so I followed him.

The year was 1990, back when America's faith-based entrepreneurs were still calling their organization the Christian Booksellers Association. That year, the CBA brought its summer retail revival up I-25 from its home office in Colorado Springs to the Colorado Convention Center in Denver. The result was the familiar marathon of music, posters, clothing, pamphlets, software, videos and the unique collection of gifts and knickknacks that insiders call "Jesus junk." If I recall, one hot trend that year was "Christian cappuccino."

The booths also offered the latest in Christian books, which flocks of public-relations specialists handed out with abandon.

That's why the elderly man was walking so slowly down the long aisles at the end of the day. Carrying books is hard work. Eventually, he stopped at a booth to take some notes, and I was able to study his face. It was the Rev. Norman Vincent Peale.

As I watched him interact with publicists, it was obvious that some of them had no idea who he was. They thought he was merely an old man who was in the way. Clearly, they didn't realize that much of the work they were doing and many of the products they were selling would not have existed if not for Peale's trailblazing work in the modern marketplace of books and mass media.

When he sat down to rest, I joined him. He recognized me, since I had interviewed him a few years earlier.

"I'm just out looking for ideas," he said. "Things keep changing, and you need to know what people are curious about. . . . I think most of the problems are the same, year after year. People are people."

Three years later, on Christmas Eve, he died at the age of 95.

In his day, Peale was a national figure who met with presidents and wrote books that offered hope to paupers. He wrote or co-wrote dozens of books, founded Guideposts magazine and delivered five decades' worth of radio commentaries.

But his legacy is one title: "The Power of Positive Thinking." This book sold 20 million copies in 41 languages and influenced legions of other writers and preachers. Half a century later, it's hard to remember why it was so controversial.

That's the thing about books, you see. They contain ideas that have consequences. Books influence other books and then sometimes books evolve into all kinds of things — from movies to computer games, from television shows to churches. Books burn up the charts in the present, but they can shape lives in the future.

Norman Vincent Peale wrote one such book. For better or for worse, "The Power of Positive Thinking" created a template that helped create the postdenominational world of religious publishing. Experts called Peale a theological cipher who sold "Christianity Lite," telling ordinary people what they wanted to hear, stripping the faith of tough doctrines and replacing true repentance with a not-so-healthy dose of pop psychiatry. The bottom line, they said, was the bottom line: Peale blurred the lines between faith and prosperity, between joy and success.

Peale stood his ground. Yes, he admitted that he was intensely interested in psychology and he believed that the church had to talk with modern people about their everyday lives in the modern world. He was constantly looking for the hot new subjects that people were talking about at water coolers and at home in front of their television sets. That meant talking about their jobs, families, wallets, hopes and fears. The goal, he said, was to deal with these issues in plain language, without complex religious jargon. He insisted that his work was rooted in the ancient truths of the Christian faith, but he pled guilty to avoiding lots of extra God-talk that might turn off consumers.

Once, this approach was controversial. Today, it is perfectly normal.

Walk into any postmodern bookstore, and the shelves will be packed with books that wed faith with self-esteem, fantasy, health, family, politics, romance and who knows what. Many contain shots of Christian faith, of one vague brand or another.

Others take the classic self-help formula of Peale and, in consumer-friendly phrases that sound few alarms, baptize it in the doctrines of other world religions or blend Christianity and other faiths into one easy-to-swallow cocktail.

This works. Ask Oprah and her many disciples.

Books contain ideas. These ideas have consequences, and they have shaped the modern marketplace, for Christians and for everyone else as well. We are shaped by ideas, especially those that mold our lives, stories and dreams.

WALKING WITH C.S. LEWIS

November 1998

He always took the early, slow train from Oxford, so he could say his prayers and enjoy the scenery before he arrived at the tiny station at the foot of the Malvern Hills.

C.S. Lewis rarely tinkered with the details of these trips, since the goal was always the same — to walk and talk with friends. He wore a rumpled tweed jacket with the obligatory leather elbow patches, baggy wool pants, walking shoes and an old hat. He had a battered rucksack, and he never carried a watch.

His host was George Sayer, his former pupil at Oxford's Magdalen College and a close friend for three decades. They usually walked the 10-mile Malvern Ridge, with its lovely views of the distant Welsh hills, the Severn Valley and the Cotswolds. But sometimes they strayed elsewhere, joined by colleagues.

"Beauty was so important to Jack, and so was good conversation," said Sayer, using the nickname Lewis preferred. "What could be better than putting the two together? One could not have found a better walking companion."

Sayer gazed out the sunny garden window in his sitting room, which served as the starting point for their travels. Then he laughed out loud.

"You should have seen Jack trying to walk with J.R.R. Tolkien! Once Jack got started, a bomb could not have stopped him, and the more he walked, the more energy he had for a good argument," said Sayer. "Now Tolkien was just the opposite. If he had something to say, he wanted you to stop so he could look you in the face. So on they would go, Jack charging ahead and Tolkien pulling at him, trying to get him to stop — back and forth, back and forth. What a scene!"

That was long ago. It has been nearly a quarter of a century since Sayer led Malvern College's English department and a decade since he wrote "Jack: C.S. Lewis and His Times." This year, fragile health prevented Sayer from fully participating in events marking the centenary of Lewis' birth on Nov. 29, 1898. Lewis died on Nov. 22, 1963, the same day as President John F. Kennedy.

It's hard to say why Lewis remains such a dominant figure, said

Sayer. The former atheist did have a unique ability to handle tough questions in a way that was both intellectual and popular. Lewis also wrote many different kinds of books — from children's literature to apologetics, from science fiction to literary criticism. Readers start reading one form of his writings, such as "The Chronicles of Narnia" fantasies, and then graduate to another, such as the more philosophical "The Problem of Pain." Many have been drawn to his work through two movies called "Shadowlands," based on the story of the Oxford don's marriage to American poet Joy Davidman.

Much of this "would have infuriated Jack because he rejected all attempts to analyze writers by dwelling on their personal lives," said Sayer. "He called this the 'personal heresy.' It is very ironic that so many people have such an astonishing attachment to C.S. Lewis as a person, or to the person that they perceive him to have been."

This trend began during the writer's lifetime. Lewis was, of course, thankful that millions embraced his work. But Sayer said he grew frustrated that so many readers — especially Americans — hailed him as a celebrity yet failed to dig deeper into the issues that most challenged him.

Lewis would probably be distressed, said Sayer, to discover that the books that made him an effective apologist in the 1940s and '50s are so popular decades later. He would ask why mainline Catholic and Protestant writers now attack Christian orthodoxy, rather than defend it. Lewis would ask why so many evangelicals keep writing books for the people already in pews, instead of focusing on those outside the church.

"Jack was a highly intellectual man, yet he was also very emotional," said Sayer. "The man I knew was highly persuasive, quite comical and very entertaining. Above all, he loved a good argument, and he rarely passed up a chance to jump into the thick of things. He would want his admirers to take his work and push on, not to stay in the same place."

HARRY POTTER AND FREE WILL

November 1999

Harry Potter had just triumphed in another face-to-face showdown with the forces of evil — represented, logically enough, by a gigantic serpent.

But the young wizard also discovered darkness, as well as light, in his own soul. His ordeal in the Chamber of Secrets revealed that he truly was free to have embraced evil and the house of Salazar Slytherin, rather than the noble house of Godric Gryffindor.

"It is our choices, Harry, that show what we truly are, far more than our abilities," says Albus Dumbledore, headmaster of the Hogwarts School of Witchcraft and Wizardry.

This kind of scene is typical of the vaguely moral, "good versus evil" plots in many fantasy novels, said literary critic Kathryn Lindskoog, who is best known for her books about the Christian apologist C.S. Lewis. Yet the Harry Potter books also specifically address the complex and confusing world of modern childhood. The characters are tempted to do what is wrong, as well as challenged to do what they know is right. They face real choices.

"The Harry Potter books are cute and naughty in that us-versus-them sort of way that kids like so much, and I guess it is true that they contain some moral ambiguities," said Lindskoog. "Welcome to the real world. The question is whether these books tell children that they are supposed to choose good over evil. It seems to me that, so far, they are doing just that."

One thing is certain: Millions of people are choosing to invite Harry Potter and his friends into their homes. "Harry Potter and the Sorcerer's Stone," "Harry Potter and the Chamber of Secrets" and

"Harry Potter and the Prisoner of Azkaban" recently grabbed the top three slots on the U.S. hardback fiction bestseller lists at the same time. British author Joanne Kathleen Rowling has promised four more books in the series.

The books have their critics. Some worry that they are too violent, and since Rowling has said future volumes will be darker and more complex, they are likely to become bloodier and more distressing. Others believe that the books may popularize witchcraft, in an era in which the principalities and powers of public education and popular culture would certainly reject, let's say, "Harry Potter and the Rock of Ages."

Nevertheless, evangelical activist Charles Colson and his radio-commentary researchers have concluded, "The magic in these books is purely mechanical, as opposed to occultic. That is, Harry and his friends cast spells, read crystal balls and turn themselves into animals — but they don't make contact with a supernatural world." Meanwhile, the characters learn "courage, loyalty and a willingness to sacrifice for one another — even at the risk of their lives. Not bad lessons in a self-centered world."

Fantasy fiction often causes controversy, stressed Lindskoog, because it blends powerful emotions and messages with symbols and stories that are wide open to different interpretations. But there are common themes that grace the classic fantasy novels. In an updated edition of her book "How to Grow a Young Reader," which surveys 1,800 works of children's literature, Lindskoog and co-author Ranelda Mack Hunsicker note that these works consistently:

- Emphasize the importance of personal choices.
- Focus on the "heroic thoughts and deeds of seemingly ordinary characters."
- Recognize the "presence of evil in the world and the need for vigilance on the part of those who love truth."

- Help the reader achieve a "clearer understanding of oneself and society without resorting to preaching."
- Provide a sense of hope.

The jury remains out on Harry Potter, said Lindskoog. But this frenzy is typical of the media fads that sweep through youth culture, including children's literature. Meanwhile, researchers continue to find increasing numbers of adolescents with cable-era television and VCRs in their rooms and, in 1998, 66 percent of American movies were rated R or worse.

"There is real evil out there, and parents need to stay on guard," said Lindskoog. "So I hope parents are out there reading the Harry Potter books for themselves and discussing them with their kids. Anything that pushes parents to get more involved in the lives of their children can't be all bad."

JOHN GRISHAM'S PULPIT

March 2000

Something mysterious happened in the wilds of Brazil when the morally bankrupt lawyer Nate O'Reilly finally found missionary Rachel Lane, the illegitimate heir of one of America's richest men.

She didn't want $11 billion. Instead, she wanted him to repent, be healed of his alcoholism and claim an outrageous gift — new life. The lawyer confessed his sins and then prayed his way through a case of jungle fever. But weeks later, he sat shaking in a pew, wracked by doubt. He wept and listed his many sins, one more time.

The story continues: "Nate closed his eyes . . . and called God's name. God was waiting. . . . In one glorious acknowledgment of failure, he laid himself bare before God. He held nothing back. He unloaded enough baggage to crush any three men. . . . 'I'm sorry,' he whispered to God. 'Please help me.' As quickly as the fever had left his body, he felt the baggage leave his soul. With one gentle brush of the hand, his slate had been wiped clean."

For decades, Christian writers have called this kind of plot twist the "Billy Graham scene," referring to the moments in Graham's old movies where the music swells and the protagonist gets born again. One reason "Christian fiction" is supposed to be so bad — and non-commercial — is that the genre's unwritten rules require these zap-the-sinners conversion scenes.

These folks need a new excuse. The scene described above is from "The Testament," the 10th bestseller by John Grisham, that Southern Baptist Sunday school teacher with all the supersized sales statistics. His new legal thriller, "The Brethren," can be found anywhere on the planet — except in "Christian" bookstores.

So far, three of his 11 novels include conversions of this sort, said Grisham during an "Art and Soul" conference at Baylor University in Waco, Texas. The novelist rarely speaks publicly — his family lives quietly on farms near Charlottesville, Va., and Oxford, Miss. — and he knew his appearance in such a high-profile Southern Baptist venue would take him into the tense turf between the Bible and the New York Times bestseller list.

"I am a Christian who writes novels. I'm not a Christian writer," he explained. "I'm not writing Christian literature. When I was a lawyer, I was a Christian who was a lawyer and tried to live my faith — not just in my profession, but in everything that I would do. I think God is involved in [my writing], as with all the other aspects of my life."

When asked the source of his writing skills, Grisham noted that he studied accounting in college — drawing a roar of laughter. In law school, he emphasized tax law. He has never taken a creative writing course. But it was crucial, he said, that his mother "didn't believe in television." Instead, their family faithfully took three steps after each move — joining a Southern Baptist church, getting new library cards and finding a Little League baseball diamond. The books soaked in, and so did the sermons.

Later, Grisham's courtroom experience inspired his first novel, "A Time to Kill," especially the soul-searing testimony of a young rape victim. Church mission trips to Brazil inspired "The Testa-ment." Another church project led to "The Street Lawyer," which was written in a 51-day frenzy after a freezing night in a homeless shelter.

The key, said Grisham, is that people who want to write suspense novels have to master that craft, with all of its ironic details and elaborate plot devices. Writers either learn how to do that, or they don't. Once someone has mastered the craft, then he can try to weave in a deeper message. It rarely works the other way around.

"Sometimes when I finish a book, I know I've done the best I can do. I know the story works," he said. "I know that the people are real and their problems are real. When I finished 'The Testament,' I was very proud. I'll do more books like 'The Testament.' I go back to those themes. I can see a few coming down the road.

"But I can't do it every time out. I have to watch it, because I'm writing popular fiction and you can't preach too much."

COMIC-BOOK VISIONARIES

November 2003

LOS ANGELES — The story has everything that a comic book needs, like rippling muscles, heaving bosoms, torture, seduction, superhuman feats of strength and moments of crippling guilt.

The story builds through pages of dramatic close-ups, epic

slaughters and cosmic revelations until, finally, the hero faces his ultimate decision. Will he take a leap of faith and risk everything?

"Oh Lord God! Hear me, please. Give me strength this one last time," he prays. "I am prepared! You strengthen me, oh Lord! . . . Now let me die here with the Philistines!"

Anyone who knows comics knows what happens next in "Samson: Judge of Israel," by Mario Ruiz and Jerry Novick. What happens next is painted in giant, ragged, screaming letters that say, "GRRUUNN," "CRAACCKK," "AAAIIIEEE" and one final "WHUMP!"

The great Bible stories, such as Samson in the Book of Judges, are packed with the epic visions and good-versus-evil absolutes that fill the pages of classic comics and their modern, supercharged siblings known as "graphic novels" or works of "sequential art." But what is less obvious is that some of today's most popular and influential comic-book artists are drawing their inspiration from deep wells of faith and classic religious stories, according to Leo Partible, an independent movie producer, graphic artist and writer.

"Anyone who knows where to look can find plenty of examples of faith in the comics and the culture that surrounds them," he said. "There is darkness there, but lots of light, too."

Thus, in the influential "Superman for All Seasons," a young Clark Kent turns to his pastor for help as he struggles to discern what to do with his life and unique abilities. Hollywood writer Kevin Smith's "Daredevil" hero wrestles with guilt while leaning on his Catholic faith. The mutant X-Man Nightcrawler quotes Scripture and talks openly about sin, penance and righteousness.

The mystery of the Shroud of Turin is woven into Doug TenNapel's sprawling "Creature Tech," which probes questions about faith and science. Artist Scott McDaniel's Web site (www. scottmcdaniel.net) mixes discussions of faith and art with its pages of Nightwing, Batman and Spider-Man illustrations. The graphic novel "Kingdom Come," which helped redefine modern comics, keeps quoting the Revelation of St. John as it paints an Armageddon vision for the superheroes of the past.

The 36-year-old Partible can quote chapter and verse on dozens of other examples as he races through stacks of well-worn comics, tracing the spiritual journeys of heroes old and new. It's crucial to understand, he said, that comic books are not just for children. They are a powerful force in movies, television, animation, popular music and video games. Hollywood studies the comics.

"Comics offer a powerful combination of visual art, the written word and the imagination," he said. "For millions of people around the world, comic books are a bridge between literature and the silver screen. . . . This is where some of our most powerful myths and iconic images come from, whether you're talking about stories that were shaped by the comics — such as the work of George Lucas and Steven Spielberg — or actual comic-book stories like the X-Men and Spider-Man.

"People have to be blind not to see this trend. It's everywhere."

Meanwhile, traditional religious believers who work in the comic-book industry face the same questions as believers who work in other mainstream media, said Partible. Should they be involved in artistic projects that dabble in the occult, if that is what it takes to land a job? How much sex and violence is too much? Should they flee the mainstream and start a "Contemporary Christian Comics" subculture that produces predictable products for Bible bookstores?

It's crucial, said Partible, that traditional believers stay right where they are in mainstream comics, helping shape some of the myths and epic stories that inspire millions. They also can help young artists break into an industry that needs both new ideas and old values.

"People are looking for heroes," he said. "People are looking for answers to the big questions, like, 'What in the hell am I doing here?' I asked that question when I was a kid, and some of the comic books

I read did a better job of answering it than many of the sermons I heard from preachers back then."

READING THE SPORTING JEWS
April 2001

When scribe Jonathan Tobin selected his all-Jewish baseball team, it was tempting to pencil in Rod Carew at second base.

This would have given his fantasy Maccabees squad its third Hall of Famer, with "Hammerin'" Hank Greenberg and southpaw Sandy Koufax. When you're talking baseball holy writ, it's impossible to overlook Carew's 3,053 hits and seven American League batting titles.

The Baseball Online Library took a leap of faith and put Carew in its Jewish All-Star Team. After all, he married a Jew, and they raised their children in the faith. But Carew never converted, despite years of rumors. Thus, Tobin sent his team into cyberspace competition without Carew's .328 lifetime average.

One passionate reader reacted to the column (at JewishWorld Review.com) by saying: "OK, so he never converted. What's important is that he's still a better Jew than most of the Jews today who are not even raising their children in the faith. I say we should count him!"

Truth is, there's more to this than pundits seeking another excuse to argue about baseball and culture while enjoying a ballgame and kosher hot dogs. The search for what the Philadelphia Jewish Exponent editor calls "the sporting Jews" offers intriguing insights into the puzzle of American Jewish identity.

Jewish immigrants once yearned — like members of any religious or ethnic minority — to find their own heroes and role models in a new land. Thus, Tobin said Jews grew up watching their elders point in history books while saying, "Look! Eddie Cantor is a Jew. Look! Irving Berlin is Jewish." It was important to thrive everywhere from Main Street to Hollywood and Vine. And then there was the sports page.

Athletics wasn't even on the radar screen in the old Jewish communities of Eastern Europe, he said. But it was impossible to deny baseball's role here, especially in the thriving urban neighborhoods into which Jews moved in the cathartic, agonizing decades before and after World War II.

Millions of Jews cheered when Greenberg opted out of a 1934 World Series game that fell on Yom Kippur. Decades later, Koufax declined to pitch in the opening game of the 1965 World Series, once again on Yom Kippur. Who could have imagined living to see such open displays of pride and Jewish identity?

"What could be a better symbol of this new Jew, this Jew who was finally living in a land where he could be comfortable in his own skin, than to be able to find Jewish heroes at the ballpark? . . . I think it's hard for us to grasp how important someone like Greenberg was at that time. He was an icon of this new Jewish experience in America," said Tobin.

That was then.

Today, American Jews live in the age of Jerry Seinfeld and Joe Lieberman. Today, it's hard to imagine a time when the word *assimilate* would have sounded good to Jewish leaders. A century ago, millions of Jews were anxious to claim a new sense of identity — as Americans. Today, the question is how many will choose to claim an old identity — as practicing Jews.

The statistics are now familiar. Jews have declined from 4 percent to 2 percent of the U.S. population. While a 1990 survey — currently being updated — found 5.9 million Jews, researchers said 1.3 million practice another faith and 1.1 million claim no faith. Only 484,000 American Jews regularly attend temple or synagogue services.

While assembling his Maccabees roster, Tobin researched whether he could list current Philadelphia catcher Mike Lieberthal, who has a Jewish father. In the Phillies yearbook, he saw that the Lieberthal family picture showed them posed in front of a Christmas tree. He took that as a sign.

"There is a phrase that we use these days to describe people who convert to Judaism or step forward to publicly claim their Jewish identity. We call them 'Jews by Choice,'" said Tobin. "What we need to realize is that, in 2001, all Jews in America are 'Jews by Choice.' That is the reality of our situation. . . .

"That seems humorous, when we're talking about hunting for Jews in the major leagues. But it isn't funny, otherwise. This is serious."

ROMEO AND JULIET, BORN AGAIN

April 2002

GRAND RAPIDS, Mich. — It's hard to imagine "Romeo and Juliet" with a happy ending.

But what if William Shakespeare had been preparing his manuscript for sale in stores linked to what used to be called the Christian Booksellers Association? What changes would he have been pressured to make?

"The lovers would meet, just as before, and the parents would still disapprove. Probably one set would not be Christians at all, providing a convenient subplot of salvation," said novelist Reed Arvin, in a rollicking lecture at the 2002 Calvin College Festival of Faith and Writing.

As newlyweds, Romeo and Juliet would strive to evangelize those lost parents. Shakespeare would manfully struggle to build tension, but "the fix would be in," with a happy ending assured, said Arvin. In the final scene, Romeo's parents would be converted and, as Juliet's father leads them in prayer, the sun would break through the clouds over Verona. Amen.

"I thank my God that William Shakespeare did not write for a CBA publisher, because that version of 'Romeo and Juliet' would have been forgotten 15 minutes after the marketing plan ran out of money," said Arvin.

But Shakespeare, rather than "making his story end like an episode of the 'Love Boat,' taught us about power and young love. . . . Above all — in messages profoundly Christian — he taught us the importance of forgiveness and showed us how the sins of the fathers are visited on the next generation. The people were real, the situation was real and the stakes were real."

Arvin's lecture on "Why I Left the CBA" was a curveball at a conference that drew a wide array of Christian publishers, editors, writers and entrepreneurs. People listened, because he was a force in the CBA before he chose to exit. In addition to his books, Arvin is a skilled pianist and producer — known for years of work with singers Amy Grant and the late Rich Mullins.

But a not-so-funny thing happened when Arvin sought a Christian publisher for a legal thriller called "The Will." He said his friends liked the book but were sure that it would offend a key CBA audience. Everyone warned him not to anger the "little old ladies."

What Arvin learned is that writers can address issues of sin and salvation, but that certain sins are more offensive than others. In Christian bestsellers — such as the omnipresent "Left Behind" series by writer Jerry Jenkins and preacher Tim LaHaye — characters commit a variety of unspeakable acts of evil. No one claims that the authors have endorsed these actions. But authors go to "literary purgatory" if they violate CBA standards on sex and bad language.

"The Will" was a perfect test case, said Arvin.

The key, he explained, is that he is writing about characters that are quite normal from a secular point of view, which means that they are messed up from a Christian point of view. Thus, when writing about a high-strung, morally confused lawyer from a Chicago megafirm, Arvin faced the question of what this character would do — in real life — if he fell in love with yet another hot female. The logical question: Would he have sex with her?

"Because I am writing a work of fiction and not propaganda, I don't ask questions such as, 'What should I have this character say next in order to lead people to Christ?' Or, 'What should I have this character do in order not to offend someone?' . . . Only this: 'What would he say next? What would he do next?'"

There is a happy ending to this story. Arvin took his manuscript to Scribner and the powers that be at Simon & Schuster. They were not worried about its strong Christian subplot or that it mentioned Jesus by name — in the context of salvation, as opposed to cursing. Then Paramount bought the film rights.

"What I am finding out is that there are major, major companies in places like Hollywood that are actively searching for stuff that will speak honestly about spiritual issues and even appeal to Christian audiences," said Arvin. "But it has to be real. It can't be fake. We have to write real stories that speak to real people."

J.K. ROWLING: INKLING?

June 2003

Harry Potter froze in terror as the hellish Dementors rushed to suck out his godfather's soul.

But he was not powerless, because he had learned the Patronus charm for use against the evil ones. So the boy wizard focused on a joyful memory and shouted, "Expecto Patronum!"

Salvation arrived in the form of a dazzling silver animal that defeated the ghouls and then cantered across the surface of a lake to Harry. It was as "bright as a unicorn" but on second glance was not a unicorn. It was a majestic stag that bowed its antlered head in salute and then vanished.

If C.S. Lewis or J.R.R. Tolkien had written this scene in "Harry Potter and the Prisoner of Azkaban," literary critics and Christian apologists would know how to break the code, according to John Granger, author of "The Hidden Key to Harry Potter." They would parse the Latin charm and study author J.K. Rowling's delicate use of medieval symbolism.

"The key is that stag, which is often a Christ symbol. But she is not content to make it a stag. It's a stag that looks like a unicorn," said Granger, who teaches Latin and Greek in Port Hadlock, Wash.

"She's saying to the reader, 'A stag may be a reach for you. So I'll have it be a stag that looks like a unicorn, since that has been a universally recognized Christ symbol for ages.' It's almost, 'Let me make this clear for you.'"

But these symbols have eluded most of the readers who have bought 192 million copies of these novels in 55 languages. (Rowling requested Latin.) Now bookstores are serving up the first 8.5 million copies of the 768-page fifth volume, "Harry Potter and the Order of the Phoenix."

The usual suspects will immediately say the usual things. Many Christians will quote Bible verses condemning magic. Academics will call the book a childish confection and analyze it as media myth and pop psychology. Librarians will give thanks that children are reading — anything.

Granger believes they are missing the obvious: Rowling has baptized her work in medieval Christian symbols and themes that shape and define her tales of good versus evil. Potter's creator, he noted, received a superior education — with studies in French and classical languages at the University of Exeter — and has a working knowledge of ancient and medieval literature. She has made no effort to hide her admiration of great writers, especially Jane Austen and C.S. Lewis.

Granger has focused on Rowling's language and symbolism, in large part because of his similar studies in "Great Books" and ancient languages. He has also attempted to predict how these themes will play out in Rowling's future Potter novels.

"I started reading the Potter books as an Orthodox Christian father who had to explain to his oldest daughter why we don't read such trash," he said. "But once I started turning the pages, the University of Chicago side of me kicked in."

Take that climactic scene in "The Prisoner of Azkaban," he said. The Latin "expecto," as used in the Apostles' Creed, is best translated "to look out for" or "to long for expectantly." And "patronus" means guardian, but it can also mean "deliverer" or "savior." So Potter cries, "I look for a savior!" and a stag appears, one that looks mysteriously like a unicorn.

In the Middle Ages, noted Granger, stags were Christ symbols, in part because of the regeneration of their antlers as "living trees." A cross was often pictured in the prongs. Lewis uses a white stag in this manner in "The Chronicles of Narnia." Unicorns were also popular Christ symbols, portraying purity and strength.

Rowling repeatedly links Potter with creatures — a phoenix, griffins, centaurs, hippogriffs, red lions — used by centuries of Christian artists. Her use of alchemy symbolism taps into medieval images of spiritual purification, illumination and perfection.

None of this is accidental, he said. Anyone who cares about Potter-mania must take Rowling more seriously.

"What we are seeing is a religious phenomenon taking place in a profoundly secular, profane culture," said Granger. "J.K. Rowling is pouring living water into a desert. . . . She is mounting a head-on attack on a materialistic world that denies the existence of the supernatural, and, so far, she is getting away with it."

YES, THERE IS A MITFORD

July 2002

Just north of Columbia, S.C., there is an unincorporated community called Mitford.

As far as author Jan Karon knows, this is the only place in North America that bears the name of the mythical North Carolina mountain town she has made so famous with her novels.

The real Mitford has a Baptist church and a barbecue joint, and that's about it.

"Now what more do you need, I mean, if you really stop and think about it?" asked Karon, before letting loose with a Southern hoot and a cackle.

Yes indeed, all that the Mitford lady needs to tell most of her tales is a busy church, a gossipy diner and the people who frequent one or the other or both. She has taken these humble ingredients, slipped them into the structures of the British "village novel" and created a franchise that keeps taking small-town virtues into the uppity territory of the New York Times bestseller lists.

"Who would want to read books with no cussing, no murder, no mayhem and no sex? . . . How can something so innocuous as these Mitford books sell 10 million copies?" asked Karon, speaking at Calvin College in Grand Rapids, Mich., just before the release of "In This Mountain," the seventh Mitford novel.

"This is what I think. I think there was a wide vein of readers out there who were just waiting for someone to write a book about them, about their dreams and their lives and their values. . . . With Mitford, we look at the ordinary lives and see something extraordinary and dramatic and full of feeling and worthy to be observed."

The books revolve around Father Timothy Kavanagh, a shockingly orthodox Episcopal priest who is so behind the times that he even converts people to Christianity. Late in life, the shy bachelor marries Cynthia Coppersmith, a witty blonde divorcée who moves to Mitford to create her award-winning books for children. The surroundings yield legions of colorful characters.

Karon began writing books in the early 1990s in the picturesque town of Blowing Rock, N.C., and other pieces of Mitford can be found in her life. When she was six, she wanted to be a preacher. When she was 10, she wanted to be an author. Today she is an author who crafts the words spoken by one of America's most beloved preachers.

But the witty blonde didn't start writing until midlife, when she abandoned her career as an advertising executive and escaped to the mountains. The pain of a divorce and the sweetness of a newborn faith figure into her story as well.

Thus, her fiercely loyal readers keep asking: Is she Cynthia?

No, says Karon. Cynthia has better legs.

But the questions keep coming. Is Barnabas, the priest's Scripture-friendly dog, going to die? Now that the Appalachian urchins Dooley Barlowe and Lace Turner have grown up, will they get married? What will Dooley do with the fortune the late Miss Sadie secretly left him? Where does Uncle Billy get his corny jokes? And what is livermush, anyway?

Then there is the ultimate question. In the new novel, Father Tim crashes into his own mortality and even survives a near-death experience. Karon has promised that the next Mitford book, "Light From

Heaven," will end the series. Readers now ask: Is Father Tim going to die?

"No, he's not going to die," she said. "This is about his LIFE."

The books are relentlessly cheerful, even though Karon weaves in dark threads. There is schizophrenia and depression, greed and grinding poverty, child abuse and alcoholism, disease and death. But most of all there is faith, even though her books fly out of secular bookstores.

Karon said it would be impossible to edit out her beliefs. It would be like trying to filter a shot of brandy back out of a cup of coffee. Once they're mixed, they're mixed.

"Even if I never mentioned the name of Jesus Christ, I can't hide from you who I am," she said. "In truth, the work that has no faith is for me not a whole work. It may be an amusing or credible or clever work, but not a whole work. Faith is a critical and urgent and necessary component of human wholeness."

ALL THOSE "LEFT BEHIND" CATHOLICS
April 2004

Catholic writer Carl Olson was struggling as he led his audience through the maze of competing Christian beliefs about the second coming of Jesus.

There are premillennialists who believe Christ will reign for 1,000 years on earth. But it wouldn't be fair to lump them with the ultra-literal premillennial dispensationalists, he noted, since these camps contain bitter rifts over the timing of "the rapture." That's when the trumpet sounds, the dead rise and Christians soar to meet Christ in the air. Then there is the ancient amillennial stance, without a 1,000-year kingdom. Oh, and don't forget the postmillennialists.

Rows of middle-aged, cradle Catholics in Salem, Ore., gazed back — utterly lost.

"I was getting absolutely nowhere," said Olson. "So I finally asked them: 'How many of you have ever heard a single sermon or even some kind of talk at church about what the Catholic faith actually teaches about the Second Coming?' There were 200 or more people there, and four or five hands went up. That's what you see everywhere."

These Catholics didn't know their catechism. But many could quote chapter and verse from another doctrinal source — the "Left Behind" novels by evangelical superstars Tim LaHaye and Jerry Jenkins. This amazes Olson, who was raised in what he called a "strong, fundamentalist Protestant" home before converting to Catholicism.

The first 11 novels have sold around 50 million copies, and that doesn't include the racks of children's books, audio editions, games, comics, DVDs and music products. Now the climactic "Glorious Appearing: The End of Days" is out, complete with a warrior Christ on a white stallion leading the angelic version of shock and awe.

The powers that be at The New York Times were struck by this scene: "Tens of thousands of foot soldiers dropped their weapons, grabbed their heads or their chests, fell to their knees, and writhed as they were invisibly sliced asunder. Their innards and entrails gushed to the desert floor, and as those around them turned to run, they too were slain, their blood pooling and rising in the unforgiving brightness of God."

For millions of modern Catholics, this is more exciting than the works of Justin Martyr, Augustine and the Second Vatican Council. Olson said it's hard to know what chunk of the "Left Behind" audience is Catholic, but publicists say that 11 percent is a good estimate.

This shouldn't be foreign territory for Catholics, said Olson, author of "Will Catholics Be 'Left Behind'?" In every Mass, they say they believe Jesus will "come again in glory to judge the living and dead." Catholics are taught — along with Orthodox Christians, Lutherans, Anglicans and many others — that "the rapture" will follow a time of tribulation and happen at the Second Coming, not seven years earlier as taught in the "Left Behind" series.

But it's hard to resist thrillers in which the mysterious Book of Revelation is decoded into visions of United Nations plots, global media, Chinese armies, Israeli jets and, well, Satan running the Vatican.

"Lots of Catholics tell me that 'Left Behind' can't be bad because LaHaye and Jenkins have the pope getting raptured along with the good guys," said Olson. "They don't even notice that this pope is considered a radical because he has started preaching what sure sounds like evangelical Protestantism. In other words, he's a real Christian. The next pope turns out to be Antichrist's right-hand man."

Meanwhile, most priests and bishops are silent, said Olson. Many fear being called "fundamentalists" if they even discuss issues of prophecy and the end times. Others may not believe what their church teaches.

The Catholic bishops of Illinois did release a "Left Behind" critique, claiming, "Overall, these books reinforce an unhealthy and immature belief in a harshly judgmental God whose mercy we earn by good behavior." But Olson said too many Catholic leaders refuse to take seriously the content of the books, movies and television programs that shape the beliefs of their people.

"If you want to be a good shepherd, you have to care about this stuff," he said. "These kinds of books and movies are where most Americans — including Catholics — get their beliefs and attitudes about faith and spirituality. . . . You cannot wish these things away. They're real."

CHAIM POTOK AND STORYTELLING
March 1997

At first glance, verse 22 in Genesis, chapter 18, doesn't seem all that important.

God has just told Abraham that Sodom and Gomorrah are in big trouble. Then a strange clause in verse 22 notes that "Abraham remained standing before the Lord." It appears, says a footnote in a major commentary on Genesis, that the nomad who would become a patriarch briefly struggles with himself, debating whether it is possible to change God's mind.

"Abraham can't decide whether to be silent or to argue with God," said novelist and playwright Chaim Potok, the project's literary editor. "Finally, he decides not to walk away and he begins to argue with God. It's just a pause. But in that pause, something happens that changes everything. It's a moment that defines an individual. It defines a story, it defines a people, it defines a culture, it transforms everything. Abraham changes and, thus, we change."

It would be wonderful, said Potok, if more readers dug into these kinds of tomes to uncover the riches buried between the lines. However, the events and stories covered in the Jewish Publication Society's Torah Commentary are now part of our cultural air. Those who watch the evil Darth Vader struggle to rediscover his conscience, or who agonize along with the latest flawed protagonist in a John Grisham morality tale, are traveling in the footsteps of Abraham and other biblical characters.

"The basic assumptions of our popular culture — even 'Star Wars' or John Grisham's novels — are built on the images and the themes and the great truths of these narratives," said Potok, who is best known for novels such as "The Chosen" and plays such as "Sins of the

Father." "The big ideas, the big symbols, filter down into the popular culture and into our lives. Without Genesis, you can't have a Grisham."

However, it's unlikely that copies of scholar Nahum Sarna's massive, but surprisingly accessible, commentaries on Genesis and Exodus will appear anytime soon in airport bookracks, or find a niche on shopping mall shelves next to the wisdom of television talk-show stars. But there are times, stressed Potok, when "life presses us up against the wall," and all kinds of people feel the need to take another look at unfiltered, archetypal texts.

One of the defining characteristics of what historians call "modernity" was that "modern" people automatically distrusted ancient texts and stories. There were religious answers to life's questions and then there were scientific, or "real," answers. Now, people are talking about "postmodernism," and one of its central tenets is that science doesn't have all the answers. People who no longer believe that science is God often hunt for God elsewhere.

"What this has done is level the playing field and made the great narratives of literature, philosophy and religion as valid as any of those so-called 'modern' narratives — such as science — in terms of giving meaning to life," said Potok. "It turns out that the answers to life's big questions may not be in the bottom of a test tube. They may even be found in the pages of a book."

Meanwhile, the clock is racing toward a new millennium. On a less apocalyptic level, many postmodern people have concluded that it's impossible to find meaning without regaining a sense of family and community. For millions raised in homes that were, to one degree or another, Jewish or Christian, this means coming to terms with the Bible — the ultimate multigenerational family narrative. If they approach these texts with an open mind and an active imagination, they may be surprised, said Potok.

"This isn't 'Star Wars.' It's not that kind of fun. But at the same time, these narratives do move right along. You could even say — in movie terms — that there is a lot of jump-cutting from scene to scene and from theme to theme. You have murders, dysfunctional families, flights from danger, great battles, close calls, broken promises, brothers betraying brothers, redemption and love. And everything happens very fast."

HARRY POTTER FOR GROWN-UP BELIEVERS

July 2003

ORLANDO — Lee Hillman's nightstand contains a copy of Sir James George Frazer's classic "The Golden Bough: A Study in Magic and Religion."

It's a condensed version, not the two-volume 1890 epic or the 12-volume monument from the following decades. The single volume contains more than enough magical minutia for ordinary readers. Six dense pages will usually put Hillman to sleep.

Nevertheless, the practicing pagan keeps reading. It has helped give perspective on her other passion — reading and writing about a certain young wizard in England.

"There is no relationship set up in the 'Harry Potter' books between magic and religion," said Hillman during Nimbus 2003, the first global convention dissecting the 2,715 pages published so far in the series. "This had to be a deliberate decision by J.K. Rowling. . . . She is using literary conceits drawn from throughout Western culture."

She scanned the crowd at a panel discussion last weekend entitled "Harry Potter: Witchcraft? Pagan Perspectives." Then she said the same thing again, as a Wiccan believer and another miscellaneous pagan nodded in agreement.

"There is nothing in these books that relates magic to any particular religion," said Hillman. "There is no connection. None. None. Zero. . . . They are not really about witchcraft."

Don't misunderstand. Hillman still loves the Potter books.

That's why she was wearing a spectacular witch's hat and robe, a flash of purple that even stood out among the 600 other colorful fans at Disney's Swan Hotel. Among online Potter devotees, the 31-year-old secretary from Rochester, N.Y., is known as "Gwendolyn Grace, Minister of Magic," and she was the driving force behind the gathering.

Nimbus 2003 sprouted out of the Internet, where the "Harry Potter for Grown-ups" e-mail list has 10,000 members, and a "Fiction Alley" list dedicated to stories written by fans for other fans has 30,000 members. With this kind of reach, organizers attracted participants — about 90 percent female — from across the United States, as well as from England and Australia.

In hotel hallways, witch wannabes raised their expensive, professionally carved wands and fought imaginary duels with tickling spells and other incantations. In the lecture halls, others heard papers on everything from "Harry Potter and the First Amendment" to "Greenhouses Are for Girls, Beasts Are for Boys? Gender Characterizations in Harry Potter." There were packed sessions on so-called slash fiction in which online scribes write gay and lesbian themes into new Potter stories.

Organizers also dedicated an entire track of lectures and panels to spiritual issues, addressing topics such as "Seven Deadly Sins, Seven Heavenly Virtues: Moral Development in Harry Potter" and "Can Any Wisdom Come From Wizardry?"

Hillman and other pagan panelists were convinced that Rowling, who has said she attends the Church of Scotland and does not believe in magic, is a wonderful writer for children but is clearly not interested in witchcraft. This is not the magic in which they believe.

"There is a cause-and-effect relationship to everything in these books," said Hillman. "You say the spell, you see the effect. . . . It's like turning on a light. You flip the switch and the magic is there. That just isn't how things work."

Meanwhile, evangelical writer Connie Neal enthusiastically found echoes of biblical stories and parables in the Potter canon. Her book "The Gospel According to Harry Potter" has been banned in many Christian stores, but "this only seems to have made the secular stores more interested," she said. She keeps challenging people to set up evangelistic reading groups that mix Bible study and "Harry Potter" discussions.

A Jewish cantor found echoes of the Talmud. A Mormon speaker found strong family values. And classics teacher John Granger aired the thesis of his book "The Hidden Key to Harry Potter," arguing that Rowling has soaked her work in centuries of Christian symbolism and spiritual alchemy themes shared with Shakespeare, Milton, Blake, C.S. Lewis and countless others.

"The human person was designed for resurrection, in love. That is what we yearn for because that is how we were created," he said. "That is what these books are about. We respond to them because we are human. Rowling is using symbols and themes that have worked for centuries. And you know what? They still work."

THE GOSPEL ACCORDING TO "THE GOSPEL ACCORDING TO . . ." BOOKS

February 2003

As author of "The Gospel According to The Simpsons," Mark Pinsky is well aware that there are no sacred cows in Springfield.

So sooner or later he expects to see Lisa Simpson walk into the family room reading a book that claims to have found theological gems in some ridiculous animated series. The book will be called "The Gospel According to Itchy and Scratchy" or maybe "Smirk On: The Spiritual Journey of Krusty the Clown."

Homer will, of course, mock her mercilessly.

Pinsky's 15 seconds of cartoon immortality could even come this weekend, when the series hits its 300th episode. "The Simpsons" has been renewed through 2005, making it the longest-running U.S. sitcom ever.

"I expect to get laughed at someday and deservedly so," said Pinsky, the veteran religion writer for the Orlando Sentinel. "Anything that's worth mocking is going to get mocked on 'The Simpsons.' They don't miss much."

If that's the case, the scribes behind Homer, Marge, Bart and the gang are sure to have noticed that Pinsky is not alone. All kinds of scholars, theologians and preachers are suddenly sojourning in the once-forbidden world of popular culture — probing everything from Bob Dylan to the Brady Bunch, from Middle Earth to Mayberry, from Tony Soprano to Harry Potter.

Pinsky's next book will be "The Gospel According to Disney: Cartoon Faith and Values." After all, Orlando is Orlando.

"On one level, all of this is simply more evidence — as if more was required — of the evaporating attention span of modern Americans," he said. "Should we be embarrassed that we have to turn to popular culture in order to find ways to talk about serious religious issues? Without a doubt, yes. But this is reality."

Anyone attempting to get a handle on the faith that is soaked into TV, movies, popular music and the rest of the mass-media universe should be prepared for surprises.

Consider the case of Homer's next-door neighbor, the *über*evangelical Ned Flanders. He is the subject of endless jokes and sight gags, as well as the occasional salute since he is clearly the town's most trustworthy and compassionate citizen.

"Everyone knows that Ned lives a Christian life. But even he doesn't talk about the heart of his Christian faith," noted Pinsky. "If you asked him how he knows that he's saved and going to heaven, he would say he is saved by grace and faith in Jesus. That's how a Christian would answer. But nobody ever asks Ned that question."

Thus, "The Gospel According to The Simpsons" ultimately sounds a lot like the faith proclaimed in most mainstream media. It's the lowest-common-denominator civic faith that Pinsky summed up in five words: "Love God and do good." Another nice summary can be found in the familiar words of the Ten Commandments.

"It's ironic. You have what is clearly meant to be seen as a Christian family, going to a Christian church, constantly talking about Christian things, but the theological constant in 'The Simpsons' is Judaism," said Pinsky, who is Jewish. Anyone who pays close attention to the faith references that weave through about 70 percent of the show's episodes knows that "it teaches that people are saved by works, not by grace."

"Maybe salvation by grace isn't as funny as the Ten Commandments," he said.

This wave of "Gospel According to . . ." books is rooted in two trends. Some evangelicals are digging into popular culture because they are willing to take risks to reach new people. Meanwhile, the fading world of mainline religion is desperately trying to appeal to the young.

Everyone wants a new "starting point," said Pinsky. The key is to find "starting points" that have widespread appeal, trigger strong feelings and stand the test of time. Whether religious bureaucrats like it or not, television shows, movies and songs are where Americans invest much of their time, money and emotions.

"Popular culture, if used properly, can be a kind of wedge into the consciousness of ordinary people," said Pinsky. "All a good pastor or a youth leader or a Sunday school teacher needs is a common set of images, a language that everybody understands and stories that they already care about.

"It's up to clergy to take it from there."

FLIGHTS OF FILMED FANTASY

After a frantic dash to the production finish line, "The Lord of the Rings" director Peter Jackson and his team flew to Los Angeles in December of 2003 to endure another test — "The Return of the King" premiere and the accompanying waves of press coverage.

Midway through a siege of interviews, Jackson stood quietly in the back of a crowded elevator at the Four Seasons Hotel in Beverly Hills. He was, of course, wearing his trademark hiking shorts and a floppy polo shirt. I do not remember if he was barefoot, but the odds are good that he was. The reporters on the elevator elected not to hound Jackson in this situation, in part because we all knew that he must be exhausted. But two critics were talking about the preview they had just seen of the other big fantasy film that was coming out, the live-action "Peter Pan" from Universal Studios.

This got Jackson's attention, and he began to question them with boyish enthusiasm. He hadn't seen the film yet, and he was curious about one thing: "How good are the sword fights? I heard they were supposed to be spectacular."

Meet the real Jackson. He can command armies of technicians, artists, writers, musicians, accountants, computer geeks and actors. He can wrestle with Tolkien-sized questions about life and death and hire bright people to help him do so. But there is also the Jackson who wants to make sure his sword fights are better than the next guy's sword fights.

If you ask this man spiritual questions, what kind of answers will you get?

Truth is, not many people have tried. But in the past few years, some journalists have had the opportunity to do so. This is important, since Jackson built one of the fantasy franchises that helped shape the imaginations of millions in the past generation. It matters what Jackson believes. It matters what George "Star Wars" Lucas believes and the same goes for the likes of Larry and Andy Wachowski of "The Matrix."

Jackson and his inner circle were, to their credit, willing to face faith questions head-on. This took place, in part, through the publicity work of Grace Hill Media in Studio City, Calif.

Most press work on behalf of Hollywood blockbusters occurs in one of two settings. In one, individual artists sit down with television reporters, who are looking for flashes of personality and sound bites that producers can fit into short reports. Stations in major local markets each receive five-minute slots in which a reporter asks one or two questions. The movie personality will always make sure that he or she says the reporter's name at least once, to give the video report that "exclusive" feel that is even more important than the content. Then there are the major interviews, in which the networks and specialty shows are given more time (think Barbara Walters).

The goal is visual and emotional. Personality is everything.

In the second setting, individuals or small groups of artists do "round-table interviews" with small circles of journalists and critics from daily newspapers, wire services, magazines and Web sites. The key is that many print-media journalists need solid content from these sessions from which they can write news articles or lengthy features. We need answers to specific questions or we're in trouble.

In my case, the bar is set higher. I need to be able to ask questions that produce answers about the faith issues in these films, questions that I hope will produce quotable answers from artists who often are either hostile to religion altogether or who struggle to put their own personal beliefs into words.

During "The Return of the King" round-table sessions, I decided to focus on one question that was practical, yet had theological overtones. I asked Jackson, as well as each of the writers, actors and producers: "In the end, who destroyed the ring?" For J.R.R. Tolkien, a devout Roman Catholic, the answer was simple, yet profound — mercy destroys the ring of power, mercy and divine providence.

But this question puzzled many of the artists involved in "The Lord of the Rings." Most knew about Tolkien's beliefs but were not sure how they shaped his writing. For some, the question was boring. For others, it seemed threatening. But Jackson and his co-writers, Fran Walsh and Philippa Boyens, knew they could not tear the spiritual questions out of these books and, thus, the movies.

After all, from their perspective, the movie literally ends with a glimpse of a world to come, with the tired, torn, yet triumphant Frodo sailing off toward silver shores.

Was this a glimpse of heaven? What is heaven? As the credits rolled, these questions were impossible to avoid because Walsh, singer Annie Lennox and composer Howard Shore wrote them right into the lyrics of "Into the West," the soaring anthem that closed the series. Based on poetic quotations near the end of Tolkien's epic, it was hard to miss the longing behind lines such as, "Don't say, we have come now to the end. White shores are calling. You and I will meet again . . ."

This is clearly spiritual language, but it is hard to know precisely what it means — either to the artists or to the people sitting in the sanctuaries that we call movie theaters. One big question leads to another. What do these great flights of filmed fantasy mean to the people who watch them over and over and over?

Jackson said he was not prepared, at first, for the questions that he heard in what he called the "God room." It's rare for world-class entertainers to face these questions, because journalists rarely ask them.

So, Peter Jackson, what really happens at the end of all things?

"We looked upon the ending, really, as being a metaphor for Frodo passing the shore. . . . You were farewelling somebody who seems to be dying. I mean, he was going on to this blessed land," said Jackson. "We do certainly feel that Tolkien regarded that as being, you know, a visualization of somebody's death. You simply get on a ship and you sail out into the harbor and farewell them into this light. It's fairly obvious what Tolkien was really referring to and we tried to honor that."

That's a start.

GEORGE LUCAS, THE FORCE AND GOD

January 1997

A long time ago, in a movie multiplex not so far away, a child looked up and asked, "Mom, Dad, is the Force the same thing as God?"

Children have been asking that question for 20 years. The simple answer is yes. But this raises another question: Which god or God is at the center of the "Star Wars" universe?

The trilogy's creator was well aware that his work invaded turf traditionally reserved for parents, priests and preachers. George Lucas wrote "Star Wars" shortly after the cultural revolution of the '60s. He sensed a spiritual void.

"I wanted it to be a traditional moral study, to have some sort of palpable precepts in it that children could understand," said Lucas, in a New Yorker interview. "There is always a lesson to be learned. . . . Traditionally, we get them from church, the family, art and in the modern world we get them from the media — from movies."

Lucas set out to create a modern mythology to teach right and wrong. The result was a fusion of "Flash Gordon Conquers the Universe" and Joseph Campbell's "The Hero With a Thousand Faces," of Arthurian legends and Japanese samurai epics, of Carlos Castaneda's "Tales of Power" and the "Narnia" tales of C.S. Lewis. Along the way, Lucas sold $1.3 billion worth of tickets, and "Star Wars" merchandise sales have topped $4 billion. Now, a revamped "Star Wars" is back in theaters, to be followed by its sequels, "The Empire Strikes Back" and "The Return of the Jedi." A trilogy of "prequels" begins in 1999.

The impact of Lucas' work has led some researchers to speak in terms of a "Star Wars" generation. A modern preacher who wants to discuss self-sacrifice will be understood by more people if he refers to the death of Jedi knight Obi-Wan Kenobi, rather than that of St. Stephen.

"It was natural that my generation would latch on to these stories," said Jason Ruspini, webmaster of the unofficial "Star Wars Home Page," one of nearly 1,000 "Star Wars" Internet sites. "They were much more attractive and appropriate than the ancient myths of Judeo-Christian theology. How could these draconian and antiquated stories possibly compete with the majesty and scope of the Star Wars universe?"

Lucas grew up in the 1950s in Modesto, Calif., reading comics, escaping to movies and watching TV. Although he attended a Methodist church with his family, biographer Dale Pollock notes that he was turned off by the "self-serving piety" of Sunday school. Lucas also visited the housekeeper's German Lutheran congregation, where he was impressed by the elaborate rituals.

Traces of these experiences are woven into his work. "The message of 'Star Wars' is religious: God isn't dead, he's there if you want him to be," writes Pollock in his book "Skywalking." Lucas puts it this way: "The laws really are in yourself."

The faith in "Star Wars" is hard to label. The Force is defined as "an energy field created by all living things. It surrounds us and penetrates us." It contains both good and evil. Jedi master Yoda clearly teaches a form of Buddhism. Yet the Lucas liturgy also proclaims, "May the Force be with you," a variation on the Christian phrase "May the Lord be with you." The plot includes other symbols and themes from biblical faith. Lucas has embraced both "passive Oriental philosophies and the Judeo-Christian ethic of responsibility and self-sacrifice," according to Pollock.

Thus, some Christians hail "Star Wars" as evidence of a cultural search for moral absolutes. On the World Wide Web, others use the films as glowing icons that teach Eastern philosophy. Welcome to the theological mall.

At the end of Pollock's book, Lucas acknowledges that, by setting his goals so high, he is asking to be judged by very high standards. The creator of "Star Wars" explains that one of his least favorite fantasies is about what will happen when he dies. Perhaps, he said, he will come face to face with God and hear these words: "You've had your chance, and you blew it. Get out."

GOD, MAN, HOBBITS AND J.R.R. TOLKIEN
August 2001

In the beginning was Eru, the One, who also was called Ilúvatar.

"And he made first the . . . Holy Ones, who were the offspring of his thought, and they were with him before aught else was made. And he spoke to them, propounding to them themes of music; and they sang before him, and he was glad."

This "Great Music" went out "into the Void, and it was not void." But something went wrong. The greatest archangel, Melkor ("He who arises in Might"), became proud and rebelled. Great was his fall into evil and he became Morgoth ("Dark Enemy of the World"). His chief servant was Sauron, who created rings of power to rule the world and "One Ring to rule them all."

The rest is a long story. Like all myths, those who want to understand "The Lord of the Rings" trilogy must start at the beginning — with the author's creation story in "The Silmarillion." J.R.R. Tolkien knew what he was doing in his tale of elves, dwarves, hobbits and men.

"The Lord of the Rings," he wrote to a friend in 1953, just before book one was published, is "a fundamentally religious and Catholic work; unconsciously so at first, but consciously in the revision." Yet Tolkien also told Father Robert Murray it was his desire to stay theologically orthodox that led him to avoid being too specific, despite the biblical parallels in the creation story.

"That is why I have not put in, or have cut out, practically all references to anything like 'religion,' to cults or practices, in the imaginary world. For the religious element is absorbed into the story and into the symbolism," wrote Tolkien.

The result is a stunningly ambitious myth, yet one that lacks the clear symbolism of an allegory or parable. Believers who share Tolkien's faith can follow the roots into Catholic imagery and tradition. Clearly the evil in Middle Earth is good that has been twisted and perverted. The humble are tempted yet triumph through sacrificial love. One age passes away before a glimpse of a world to come. There is much more.

Yet millions have read an epic tale of nondoctrinal good versus undefined evil — period. It all depends on one's point of view, especially when it comes time for other artists to re-create the myth with the help of a camera lens. When "The Lord of the Rings" moves to theaters, will the myth remain centered in its creator's faith?

"Tolkien could not create from nothing. Only God can do that. But he was able to subcreate an entire world using his imagination, his beliefs and his experiences in the world around him," said British writer Joseph Pearce, author of "Tolkien: Man and Myth."

"That is certainly what he set out to do with 'The Lord of the Rings.' . . . But if you tear the myth away from Tolkien's worldview, then the story isn't going to make sense anymore. It may, literally, become incoherent — a neopagan fantasy."

This is especially true since Tolkien's work includes images and ideas drawn from legions of myths, legends and traditions. His goal was to create a myth that combined elements of others, Pearce said, "with the whole story illumined from within by a Trinitarian, Christian light."

Now, new artists will be "subcreators" of movie versions of "The Lord of the Rings" that will cut and mold 500,000 words of prose into nine hours of multiplex magic. Millions will see these movies, and most will use this lens to interpret the books — if they read or reread them. The official Web site (www.lordoftherings.net) offers no sign of Tolkien's faith or worldview.

There is no telling what may end up on the screen, Pearce said.

"The great strength of Tolkien's work may, in the end, be its weakness. He has created truth in a form that is truly sublime — myth. Yet that is also a form of art that can easily be twisted. He was writing a myth, but he wanted it to be a true myth, a myth rooted in Truth with a capital T. Take away that truth, and you change the myth."

"STAR WARS":
THE ONLY PARABLE IN TOWN

June 1999

Every epic story needs a central character, and he has to come from somewhere.

So the key moment in the cosmos of mythmaker George Lucas is when Jedi master Qui-Gon Jinn asks Shmi Skywalker to identify the father of her mysterious young son, Anakin, who will someday become the evil Darth Vader.

"There is no father," she replies, in Terry Brooks' novel "Star Wars: Episode I, The Phantom Menace," which is based on the screenplay by Lucas.

"I carried him, I gave birth to him. I raised him. I can't tell you any more than that."

It seems the slave boy was "conceived not by human contact, but by the essence of all life, by the connectors to the Force itself, the midi-chlorians," a form of life living in the blood. "Comprising collective consciousness and intelligence, the midi-chlorians formed the link between everything living and the Force," explains the novel.

This leads to the final details in this nativity story. The priestly Jedi have long pondered an ancient prophecy that "a chosen one would appear, imbued with an abundance of midi-chlorians, a being strong with the Force and destined to alter it forever." The chosen one would "bring balance to the Force" — balance between the darkness and the light.

Once upon a time, "Star Wars" raised one big question for parents and clergy: Is the Force the same thing as God? Now, the first chapter of the saga that many scholars believe has shaped a generation is raising more questions, even if Lucas scoffs at believers who dissect his work.

Why use the title "chosen one"? Was this a miraculous conception? Is Qui-Gon a John the Baptist figure? Perhaps Anakin Skywalker is the Moses who will liberate his people? If the Force is God, and the midi-chlorians help channel the Force, then what are the midichlorians? Did Lucas shred the Holy Spirit and then inject the results into his characters' bloodstreams?

"When you look at literature, you find myths and messiahs and saviors everywhere. That's fair, and everybody does that," said Alex Wainer, a Milligan College colleague of mine whose doctoral work focused on mythic archetypes in popular culture, including "Star Wars." "The problem isn't that Lucas is creating a heroic myth and using religious symbolism. But he has taken all of the religions, put them in a blender and hit the button."

While many critics will say that the gospel according to Lucas is too vague, the problem for many traditional believers will be that his story has become too detailed. The use of the virgin birth motif and the title "chosen one" may even cut through the entertainment fog that envelops most consumers when they enter a movie theater.

"Lucas is getting so specific that his work is losing its metaphor quality," said Wainer. "He isn't just using an occasional religious theme. He is creating a whole religious system, and the more questions he raises, the more he's going to have to answer. He's on the verge of demystifying his own myth, and he may end up killing the whole thing. It's like he's trying too hard."

For years, Lucas has said that his goal is to create a framework in which children can learn about good and evil, right and wrong. However, he also is painting a picture inside this frame. While he clearly believes that children need moral guidance, he also urges them to follow their emotions, not religious dogmas.

As Qui-Gon tells the young Skywalker: "Concentrate on the moment. Feel, don't think."

"I see 'Star Wars' as taking all the issues that religion represents and trying to distill them down into a more modern and easily accessible construct — that there is a greater mystery out there," Lucas told Bill Moyers in a Time interview. "I remember when I was 10 years old, I asked my mother, 'If there's only one God, why are there so many religions?' I've been pondering that question ever since, and the conclusion I've come to is that all the religions are true. Religion is basically a container for faith."

J.R.R. TOLKIEN, SIN AND CREATION
December 2002

NEW YORK — Screenwriter Philippa Boyens gets a tired look in her eyes when she recalls the surgery required to turn "The Lord of the Rings" into a movie, even a sprawling trilogy of three-hour movies.

"It's so hard," she said. "It's hard, it's hard, oh God, it's hard."

One agonizing cut in the screenplay removed a glimpse of the myth behind J.R.R. Tolkien's 500,000-word epic. In this lost scene, the traitor Saruman is torturing the noble Gandalf. "What," asks the evil wizard, "is the greatest power?" Gandalf replies, "Life."

"You fool," says Saruman. "Life can be destroyed. Did I teach you nothing?"

Trying again, Gandalf says, "Creation."

"Yes," answers Saruman, "the power to create life."

Millions of readers and now moviegoers have seen "The Lord of the Rings" as an epic tale of good versus evil.

Many have tried to pin labels on each side. The dark lord Sauron and his minions represent Nazi Germany, and the armies of Middle Earth are England and its allies. Wait, said scribes in the 1960s. The forces of evil were industrialists who wanted to enslave Tolkien's peaceful, tree-hugging elves and hobbits. The dark lord's "One Ring to rule them all" was the atomic bomb, or nuclear power, or something else nasty and modern.

The reality is more complex than that, said Boyens, after a press screening of "The Two Towers," director Peter Jackson's second "The Lord of the Rings" film.

"This is not a story about good versus evil," she said. "It's about that goodness and that evilness that is in all of us."

Anyone who studies Tolkien, she said, quickly learns that the Oxford don rejected allegorical interpretations of his work.

Nevertheless, Tolkien was a devout Catholic, and his goal was to create a true myth that offered the modern world another chance to understand the timeless roots of sin. Thus, even his darkest characters have mixed motives or have been shaped by past choices between good and evil. Even his virtuous heroes wrestle with temptations to do evil or to do good for the wrong reasons.

The dark lord Sauron, noted Boyens, "was your basic fallen angel. If you go back even further within this mythology, you have a world that begins with Ilúvatar, who is the One, who is basically God."

Ilúvatar created the world through music, noted Boyens. But one angel, Melkor, was "jealous of the power of creation" and struck a note of discord, shattering the harmony. Yet Ilúvatar did not destroy his creation. Instead, he gave his creatures the freedom to make choices between darkness and light, between evil and mercy.

It is hard to put this level of complexity on a movie screen. Nevertheless, Boyens and Jackson stressed that "The Lord of the Rings" team tried to leave the foundations of Tolkien's myth intact. The ultimate war between good and evil is inside the human heart.

"We didn't make it as a spiritual film, but here is what we did do," said Jackson, who is a co-writer and co-producer as well as the director of the project. "Tolkien was a very religious man. But we made a decision a long time ago that we would never knowingly put any of our own baggage into these films. . . .

"What we tried to do was honor the things that were important to Tolkien, but without really emphasizing one thing over another. We didn't want to make it a religious film. But he was very religious, and some of the messages and some of the themes are based on his beliefs."

The goal is to retain the timeless quality of the books, said Jackson.

Most of the filming for this three-movie project was done before the events of Sept. 11, 2001, he noted. The director had no way to know his movies would reach theaters during such tense times. Once again, many want to match headlines with events in Tolkien's masterwork.

"You sort of get the impression — which can be depressing — that Tolkien's themes really resonate today and that they're probably going to resonate in 50 years and then in 100 years," said Jackson. "I don't think humans are capable of actually pulling themselves out of these basic ruts."

GOD-TALK AFTER "THE MATRIX": POP GNOSTICS

May 2003

The words of the scripture are clear: Everything changes when someone is born again.

"Before his first or physical birth, man was in the world of the matrix. He had no knowledge of this world; his eyes could not see; his ears could not hear. When he was born from the world of the matrix, he beheld another world," wrote Abdul Baha, son of the Bahai prophet Baha'u'llah, nearly a century ago. Truth is, "the majority of people are captives in the matrix of nature, submerged in the sea of materiality."

When freed, they gain a "transcendent power" and ascend to a higher kingdom.

Perhaps even to Zion.

Wait a minute. Does this mean that millions of moviegoers lining up at 8,400-plus theaters to see "The Matrix Reloaded" will witness the Bahai version of a Billy Graham movie? Or is this trilogy a door into a kung fu vigilante Buddhism?

Or is it some kind of neo-Christian parable?

The World Wide Web is jammed with sites offering precisely that spin. Isn't Keanu Reeves playing a superhacker called Neo, a messiah whose coming was foreseen by the prophets, a Christ figure who is reborn, baptized, murdered and resurrected? Isn't his real name Thomas Anderson (Greek "andras" for man, thus "son of man")? Doesn't a character named Trinity save him?

Acolytes have compiled pages of similar references. Isn't Neo's teacher Morpheus a John the Baptist figure? Why is their ship called the Nebuchadnezzar? And it's a "Mark III, no. 11." Perhaps that is Mark 3:11, which says of Jesus, "Whenever the unclean spirits saw him, they fell down before him and cried out, 'You are the Son of God.'"

There will be plenty of fresh clues in "The Matrix Reloaded" and the upcoming "The Matrix Revolutions." When it comes to spiritual goodies, this franchise that critics call the "R-rated 'Star Wars'" has something to intrigue or infuriate everyone, from Hollywood to the Bible Belt.

No one questions the impact of "The Matrix," which grossed $170 million in the United States, $460 million worldwide and influenced countless movies, computer games, music videos and commercials. But the devotion of its true believers is revealed in another statistic. It was the first DVD to sell more than 1 million copies.

Meanwhile, Andy and Larry Wachowski have religiously avoided doing interviews that might dilute the mystery surrounding their movie.

But a fan in a Warner Home Video online chat session did manage to ask: "Your movie has many and varied connections to myths and philosophies: Judeo-Christian, Egyptian, Arthurian and Platonic, just to name those I've noticed. How much of that was intentional?"

To which the brothers replied, "All of it." While calling their beliefs "nondenominational," they did confirm that Buddhism plays a major role in "The Matrix." When asked if their work was shaped by the ancient Christian heresy called Gnosticism, they cryptically replied, "Do you consider that to be a good thing?"

While the first film draws images and details from many conflicting traditions, its worldview is deeply rooted in Eastern religions, especially Buddhism and Gnosticism, according to Frances Flannery-Dailey of Hendrix College and Rachel Wagner of the University of Iowa. Clearly, the big idea is that humanity's main problem is that it is "sleeping in ignorance in a dream world" and the solution is "waking to knowledge and enlightenment."

Writing in the Journal of Religion and Film, they note that the Gnostic messiah brings salvation through a secret truth that lets believers wake up and escape the shabby reality that surrounds them. Through training in the discipline of "stillness," this savior learns that what appears to be the real world is an illusion he can manipulate with his will. It's a gospel of esoteric knowledge, not repentance and grace.

But Wagner and Flannery-Dailey ask: Where are the Gnostic gods in "The Matrix"?

"Divinity may . . . play a role in Neo's past incarnation and his coming again as the One. If, however, there is some implied divinity in the film, it remains transcendent, like the divinity of the ineffable, invisible supreme god of Gnosticism, except where it is immanent in the form of the divine spark in humans."

GOD-TALK AFTER "THE MATRIX": THEOLOGY FOR SALE

May 2003

Predicting the future is dangerous, especially when a would-be prophet puts her thoughts in writing.

But that's what author Phyllis Tickle did two decades ago when she wrote, "Books are about to become the portable pastors of America." That turned out to be true. Now, in light of "The Matrix," she is updating that prophecy about how Americans talk about faith.

It helps to flashback to a statistical earthquake that rattled the book business.

In 1992, the company that dominates sales to libraries saw a stunning 92 percent rise in its religious trade. Then in 1994, religious sales by the giant Ingram Book Group soared 246 percent. In a few years, this niche grew 500 percent, said Tickle, who has covered this trend for Publishers Weekly and in several of her two dozen books.

The growth was "malignant," she said. "Bookstore owners kept telling me people would vanish into that back corner where the religious shelves were and stay for hours. When they did that, you just knew they should have been going to see their pastors. But they weren't doing that."

These seekers didn't buy into doctrines and denominations. They didn't want "theology." They wanted new ideas, images and spiritual stories. They wanted what Tickle began calling "God-talk," and millions started finding it with the help of cappuccino and Oprah.

And in 1999, everything changed again.

"When 'The Matrix' came out, it became the best treatise on God-talk that has ever been made," said Tickle. "It could not have been done with a book. It could not have been done with words. . . . The primacy of place in creative, cutting-edge God-talk has shifted from nonfiction in the 1980s to fiction in the 1990s, and now it is shifting again to the world of the visual, especially to the kinds of myths and stories we see in movies such as 'The Matrix.' We're talking about the manipulation of theological fantasies, and this is a natural fit for visual media."

"Theology," she said, is found in the world of doctrine, history, academic credentials and ecclesiastical authority. But "God-talk" thrives far from most pulpits. Its standards are flexible, evolving, user-defined and rooted in small communities. This is a true "democratization of theology," she said, and can be seen as an extension of Protestantism's division into thousands and thousands of independent denominations, movements and churches.

But God-talk leaders are more likely to work in popular media than in religious institutions. As creators of "The Matrix" trilogy, Andy and Larry Wachowski are touching millions of lives. The first film grossed $460 million worldwide and shaped countless movies, computer games, music videos and commercials. "The Matrix Reloaded" — on a record 8,517 screens — topped $130 million at the box office in its first four days. "The Matrix Revolutions" completes the cycle.

Writing in the Journal of Religion and Film, James L. Ford of Wake Forest University argues that these films offer a powerful fusion of themes from Buddhism, clashing brands of Christianity, Greek mythology, cyberculture and legions of other sources.

"It is impossible to know what narratives will become the foundation myths of our culture," noted Ford, in his "Buddhism, Christianity and 'The Matrix'" essay. "But epic films like 'The Matrix' are the modern-day equivalent of 'The Iliad,' '[The] Odyssey' . . . or various biblical myths. Indeed, one might well argue that popular films like 'The Matrix' and 'Star Wars' carry more influence among young adults than the traditional religious myths of our culture."

Tickle can trace this trend for decades, from the generic God of Alcoholics Anonymous to the nearly generic God of "Touched by an Angel," from the rise of the self-help publishing industry to waves of immigration that brought the mysteries of Eastern religion to Hollywood.

Mainstream religious leaders can argue about the ultimate meaning of all this, she said. But they cannot ignore it.

"The Matrix" has "posited a new theological framework," she said. "Now we have to find out the details. What is the primal cause for this world? Where is God? Who is God? Does what is going on in these films support or oppose a basic Judeo-Christian approach to morality? We don't know the answers to these questions yet."

TRUST YOUR FEELINGS, DARTH?

June 2002

No wonder Anakin Skywalker seems so confused.

Every time the Jedi apprentice turns around, a spiritual master tells him to trust his feelings, search his feelings or follow his feelings. Trouble is, the young superwarrior in "Star Wars: Attack of the Clones" is a tornado of feelings. He feels love. He feels hate, ambition, desire, frustration, fear and fury.

Yet when he follows his heart, the Jedi tell him to set aside his desires and do his duty.

Well, do feelings trump duty, or is it the other way around?

"I don't know what it says in the Jedi handbook, but it's obvious that George Lucas hasn't answered this question," says Catholic writer Roberto Rivera, who is best known for his pop-culture research for evangelical leader Chuck Colson.

"It's especially interesting that the characters that represent the good side of the Force — like Obi-Wan Kenobi — stress the importance of following your feelings. But the characters that represent the dark side — like Chancellor Palpatine — are also telling Anakin he must learn to trust his feelings. Why do the good guys and the bad guys agree with each other?"

This may sound like the geeky "Star Wars" nitpicking that thrives in cyberspace, where legions of Lucas acolytes circulate catechisms detailing how many Jedi can twirl on the point of a light saber. But these are not meaningless questions for the generations baptized in images from the original trilogy and its sequels.

Like it or not, what Lucas says about God and man is important.

"Star Wars is the closest thing many Americans have to a myth — by which I mean the stories that help us make sense of our lives and the world around us, and the traditional means by which cultures transmit their values and beliefs," argues Rivera, in a Boundless.org essay called "Love, Sacrifice and Free Will in Star Wars."

Thus, it matters if Lucas has created a myth that makes any sense, even on its own terms. It matters if the Force provides a coherent framework for the actions of his characters. It matters if Lucas is stuck somewhere between karma and Calvinism, spinning morality tales in a universe ruled by an impersonal "energy field created by all living things" that somehow has a will and a plan for the souls it controls.

After all, notes Rivera, it "was Lucas who called 'Star Wars' the story of a man's fall from grace and his subsequent redemption. These are terms with moral, if not religious, significance."

The key is that Lucas created a pop faith the same way he created his monsters. He took the head of one creature, attached it to the body of another, stuck on the tail of something else and enlarged the result to awesome size.

"I didn't want to invent a religion," Lucas once told journalist Bill Moyers. "I wanted to try to explain in a different way the religions that already existed. . . . I put the Force into the movie in order to try to awaken a certain kind of spirituality in young people — more a belief in God than a belief in any particular religious system."

The bottom line: "The conclusion I have come to is that all the religions are true."

Yet Lucas wanted an epic story of good and evil, darkness and light. His films center on the life of an anointed one who will "bring balance" between the yin and the yang of the Force, yet Lucas never defines his terms. He never says what is good and what is evil and why. Heroes and villains alike have to follow their feelings.

"There is zero evidence in the 'Star Wars' films that anyone is ever taught anything about what is right and what is wrong," notes Rivera. "We don't even know why the dark side is dark. It's a mystery. It's a concept with no meaning. . . .

"Everybody is supposed to do the right thing, but nobody wants to stop and give any serious thought as to how a person is supposed to know what is the right thing to do. That is a rather important question to leave unanswered, if you stop and think about it."

VAGUE FAITH IN MIDDLE EARTH
December 2003

LOS ANGELES — Faced with the end of his world, even the cheery hobbit Pippin lost hope.

"I didn't think it would end this way," he tells Gandalf, as they watch the forces of evil advance in Peter Jackson's epic "The Return of the King."

"End? No, the journey doesn't end here," replies the wizard, who has already had one near-death experience and has been reborn. "There's another path, one that we all must take. The grey rain-curtain of this world rolls back and it will change to silver glass and then you see it."

Confused, Pippin asks, "See what?"

With a wry smile, Gandalf replies, "White shores and beyond them, a far green country under a swift sunrise."

This speech is based on some of J.R.R. Tolkien's beautiful language at the end of "The Lord of the Rings" and poetically expresses his belief in a life to come.

Yet there are other ways to interpret this scene and the whole 500,000-word trilogy, noted the actor inside those wizard's robes. As an openly gay atheist, Sir Ian McKellen said he had no problem putting his own spin on Tolkien's visions. The key, he said, is that this is a work of cultural myth, not Christian allegory.

"The interesting thing about Hobbiton to me is that it doesn't have a church," said McKellen, during a blitz of interviews hours before the premiere of "The Return of the King" in Los Angeles. "It's appealing to me that people like these stories, and yet there isn't an archbishop and there isn't a pope telling you what to believe. . . .

"Despite being a Catholic, I don't think he was trying to write a Catholic parable, so I don't think we were meant to draw conclusions about faith from it. But I am sure that other people disagree."

Yes, they certainly do, and the global success of these movies — $3 billion at the box office is a safe guess — only raises the stakes in such debates.

Many Christians quickly quote Tolkien's claim that his trilogy was a "fundamentally religious and Catholic work." Others criticize its lack of clear, evangelistic Christian content and distrust his love of magic and myths. Meanwhile, some readers prefer to embrace its elves, wizards and back-to-nature themes.

Almost everyone involved in the movies believes "The Lord of the Rings" contains "spiritual" or even "sacred" themes. But they struggle to define these words.

Facing a circle of reporters from religious publications, members of Jackson's team emphasized that they strove to avoid personal agendas that might betray Tolkien. Yet they also stressed they did not believe Tolkien had a dogmatic agenda.

The central "tenet that is underlying the story is his Catholicism, which is at the heart . . . of the book," said Fran Walsh, a producer, screenwriter and mother of two children with Jackson. "In the end, if there is anything to be taken from the film it's that it's about faith." The story is also about death and the knowledge that its heroes "will endure in some form" after their passage to another land, she said.

So this is a story about "faith," "hope," "courage," "decency," "sacrifice," and even eternal life. It's about the triumph of "simple goodness." But it is not, as screenwriter Philippa Boyens put it, about moral absolutes that proclaim: "This is good and this is evil! And this is what you must do!"

Yet the final outcome — the destruction of the "One Ring of power" — depends on key characters making agonizing choices between good and evil.

The tormented Gollum chooses poorly and reaps what he has sown. The noble Frodo chooses poorly as well, yet he is saved by his earlier acts of compassion toward Gollum.

"It was Frodo's destiny to accept this ring," said Elijah Wood, who plays Frodo. "But it's Frodo's mercy that actually destroys the ring. The ring is not destroyed by any person's will. I mean, it is the will of Frodo that gets it to where it needs to go. But it is indeed his mercy for Gollum that allows Gollum to meet them at the Crack of Doom and to stop Frodo."

The whole thing, said Wood, is "a bit of a puzzle piece."

The movie's director was asked if the word "providence" might apply to this mystery.

"Yes," said Jackson.

"CONSTANTINE": AND ALL THE PEOPLE SAID, "WHOA"

February 2005

LOS ANGELES — Hell looks really cool, when seen through a Hollywood lens.

The good guys in the thriller "Constantine" do comment on the sulfur smell in the hell edition of Los Angeles, and it's a pain coping with all those extra tortured, brainless, flesh-eating demons on the 101 Freeway. But the city still looks like Los Angeles, even after an eternity of hurricane-force firestorms.

The other place can't compete, when it comes to entertainment value.

"The reason why heaven isn't shown as much in these kinds of movies, honestly, is that no one knows how to depict it in a cool way," said screenwriter Frank Cappello, after the film's press screenings.

"Audiences love to see hell. They want to see demonic images. But if you show them angelic beings, if you show them the light . . . it's like they say, 'Oh, gosh.'"

So it's no surprise that "Constantine" offers a mere glimpse of a heavenly reward, before its chain-smoking, hard-drinking, cussing anti-hero is yanked back to his life as a rock 'n' roll exorcist. The John Constantine character was born in stacks of "Hellblazer" comic books and, as played by the neomessianic Keanu Reeves, is part

Dirty Harry and part Indiana Jones, channeling "The Matrix" and "Men in Black."

How dark is this movie? The angel Gabriel gets ticked off at humanity and decides to cue the apocalypse.

The director and writers agreed that their movie raises big questions about salvation and damnation, sin and repentance, fate and free will. It will raise eyebrows among the 81 percent of Americans who, according to a 2004 Gallup poll, believe in heaven and the 70 percent who believe in hell.

"I'm a skeptic, myself," said director Francis Lawrence. "For all I know, you die and rot in a box and that's it."

This response was par for the course, as the "Constantine" cast and crew fielded questions from critics and reporters, including a roomful of Catholic and Protestant writers. One after another, the Hollywood professionals said they wanted their movie to inspire questions but remain agnostic about answers.

A Catholic priest among the press agreed that it doesn't make sense to expect coherent doctrine from a horror movie, even one this packed with references to Catholic rituals, relics and art. Yet "Constantine" is precisely the kind of pop-culture event that may cause young people to ask questions.

"It's based on a comic book and looks like a video game," said Father Joe Krupp of FaithMag.com and Lansing (Mich.) Catholic High School. "Like it or not, you just know that the kids are going to be talking about this, and we need to pay attention. . . .

"This movie is messy, but it does say that there is a heaven and a hell, and it says that our choices are powerful and matter for eternity. It also says that each of us was created by God for a purpose. It says that several times."

Spiritual warfare is quite literally the key, with the anti-hero fighting to earn his way into heaven. At one point, Constantine chants Latin prayers and threatens to send the demonic Balthazar to heaven instead of hell in a brass-knuckles version of Last Rites. But just before he pulls the trigger — on a shotgun shaped like a cross — he reminds his adversary that he must "ask for absolution to be saved."

Constantine knows how to get to heaven, stressed Cappello. He is simply too angry and cynical to obey. Seek God's forgiveness? Forget about it.

"His pride gets in the way of him asking to be let off the hook," said Cappello. "It's basically, 'I'm going to do it myself.'"

Yet Reeves urged moviegoers not to judge his world-weary character too harshly, because he does muster up one act of self-sacrifice. In the "secular religiosity" of this film, that is enough.

"That's what, you know, gives him a chance of going upstairs," said Reeves. "But . . . did he make the sacrifice so that he could go to heaven, or does he really mean it?" In the end, "the man upstairs knows, just like Santa Claus, if you're telling a lie or if you're really nice. He knows."

And all the people said, "Whoa."

"THE MATRIX": THE APOCALYPSE

October 2003

Anyone looking for "The Matrix" movies at a video store knows to seek the digital mythologies shelved under "science fiction."

That will have to do, since there isn't a space labeled "apocalyptic."

"These movies are truly that ambitious," said the Rev. Chris Seay, co-author of "The Gospel Reloaded," about faith and "The Matrix" phenomenon. "This story reads more like the Book of Revelation more than it does your normal sci-fi thriller. Everything has this other layer of meaning. . . . You have to wrestle with all that symbolism and philosophy if you take these movies seriously."

That statement may sound ridiculous to most clergy, said Seay, pastor of the young Ecclesia congregation in urban Houston. But anyone who studies Hollywood knows that the release of "The Matrix Revolutions" will be an event of biblical proportions to millions.

The numbers are staggering. The final movie in the trilogy will open — zero hour is 9 a.m. in New York City — on almost 20,000 movie screens in 60-plus nations. Meanwhile, Forbes estimates gross revenue for "The Matrix" and "The Matrix Reloaded" is almost $2 billion, when ticket sales are combined with video games, music, DVDs and other merchandise.

It matters little that Andy and Larry Wachowski veered into "Star Wars" limbo in "Reloaded," sinking into a swamp of linguistics and logic while striving to explain the visual mysteries of "The Matrix." Few acolytes blinked when Larry Wachowski left his wife, hooked up with a dominatrix and, newspapers reported, began taking hormones to prepare for a sex-change operation.

Millions will flock to theaters anyway.

"Everything about these movies is getting bigger — bigger action scenes, bigger philosophical speeches, bigger rumors," said Greg Garrett, co-author of "The Gospel Reloaded" and an English professor at Baylor University. "Now they have to justify the buzz. . . . I have faith that these guys are talented enough storytellers that they will be able to create some kind of cosmology that ties all this together."

But anyone seeking one coherent set of answers has got the wrong trilogy. The only certainty in "The Matrix" universe is that its new path to enlightenment is made out of pieces of all of the older paths, even if they contradict each other. The only absolute truth is that there is no one absolute truth, no one true faith.

Instead, these movies offer a crossroads where "all of our stories collide," write Seay and Garrett. "They not only coexist, they come together to create a story of tension, adventure and spiritual pursuit. As Buddhism, Christianity, Zen, existentialism, Gnosticism, Plato and Jacques Derrida interact with one another, we are encouraged to interact with them as well."

This shouldn't surprise anyone who has studied religious trends in recent generations, they added. "If movie theaters have become the new cathedrals, as cultural observers from Bill Moyers to George Lucas argue, then the priests of that domain are clad in black leather. And Cool Hand Luke, Obi-Wan Kenobi and E.T. assist in serving the sacrament."

Yes, "The Matrix" is this kind of metaphysical myth, said actor Laurence Fishburne, who plays a Batman meets John the Baptist hero named Morpheus. Many viewers will seek, and find, deep meaning in the ties that bind Morpheus, the heroine named Trinity and the messianic Neo.

"What kids or young people will get from this divine trinity is . . . not for us to say," he said at a Warner Bros. press conference. "If they get whatever they need, then we've done proper service not just to the filmmakers but the larger thing, which is the story itself. So there you have it."

So there you have what, precisely?

"The Matrix" movies show miracles, but no ultimate power that performs them. Characters make moral choices but follow no commandments. They pray, but to an undefined god. They believe, but in what?

"We deal with all kinds of people today," said Seay, "who believe in a Creator, but they have no idea how to articulate that belief. Their God is energy or light or love or something. But it's real to them, and they don't want to answer that question. . . . 'The Matrix' movies are powerful because they offer people all kinds of things to believe in, and none of them are very specific."

THE VISIONS OF TOLKIEN AND JACKSON

January 2005

If J.R.R. Tolkien didn't know the perfect word to describe something, he often created his own word or even a completely new language.

The climax of "The Lord of the Rings," he decided, was a "eucatastrophe" — which calls to mind words such as "Eucharist" and "catastrophe." The scholar of ancient languages defined this as a moment of piercing joy, an unexpected happy ending offering a taste of God's Easter triumph over sin and death. Tolkien thought this sacramental element was at the heart of his new myth.

Thus, Greg Wright of HollywoodJesus.com asked Peter Jackson how members of his team handled this in their movie trilogy. When they wrote the scene in which the one ring of power is destroyed, did they discuss Tolkien's theory of "eucatastrophe"?

"No," replied Jackson. "What's it mean?"

It wasn't a normal Hollywood question, but Wright wasn't involved in normal press-tour interviews. In 2002 and 2003, Jackson and other artists behind the films sat down for round-table discussions with religion-news specialists and critics from religious media. The questions ranged from the nature of evil to computer-generated monsters, from salvation to elvish poetry.

Now the extended edition of "The Return of the King" is done, and the trilogy is complete, at least until some future extended-extended anniversary set. For Wright and other Tolkien experts, it's time to ask how these movies have changed how future generations will perceive these classic books.

Jackson and his co-writers, Fran Walsh and Philippa Boyens, knew that Tolkien's traditional Catholic faith had deeply influenced

"The Lord of the Rings." Their goal was to keep the "spirit of Tolkien" intact, while producing films for modern audiences. They said they had vowed not to introduce new elements into the tale that would clash with Tolkien's vision.

"You would have to say that these are extremely gifted people and that they showed incredible dedication and integrity," said Wright. "But the questions remain: What is the spirit of Tolkien? How well do Jackson, Walsh and Boyens understand the spirit of Tolkien?"

It helps to know that Tolkien never expected these books to reach a mass audience. He thought they would appeal to his friends and scholars, who would quickly recognize his Catholic images and themes. In his book "Tolkien in Perspective," Wright argues that the author eventually realized that millions of readers were missing the point.

Now, millions and millions of people are seeing what Tolkien called his "fundamentally religious and Catholic work" through the lens of artists who knew the importance of his beliefs, but did not share them. Wright discusses these issues at length in his new book, "Peter Jackson in Perspective."

Take, for example, Tolkien's conviction that all true stories must somehow be rooted in the reality of evil, sin and the "fallenness" of humanity.

Jackson was blunt: "I don't know whether evil exists. You see stuff happening around the world and you believe it probably does. . . . I think that evil exists within people. I don't know whether it exists as a force outside of humanity."

Walsh and Boyens emphasized that the books are about faith, hope, charity and some kind of life after death. What about sin?

"You don't fall if you have faith," said Boyens, and true faith is about "holding true to yourself" and "fellowship with your fellow man." "The Lord of the Rings," she said, is about the "enduring power of goodness, that we feel it in ourselves when we perceive it in others in small acts every day. . . . That gives you reason to hope that it has significance for all of us as a race, as mankind, that we're evolving and getting better rather than becoming less, diminishing ourselves through hatred and cruelty. We need to believe that."

These noble sentiments do not match the beliefs that inspired Tolkien, said Wright. In these interviews, similar misunderstandings emerged on Tolkien's beliefs about truth, providence, salvation, death, heaven and hell. However, commentaries and documentaries included in the final "The Lord of the Rings" DVD set do address some of these issues from Tolkien's perspective, including that mysterious concept of "eucatastrophe."

"I think that you can find Tolkien's vision in these movies if you already know where to look," said Wright. "But if you don't understand Tolkien's vision on your own, you may or may not get it."

STAR CULTURE WARS
May 2005

While tweaking the original "Star Wars" movie for rerelease, director George Lucas decided that he needed to clarify the status of pilot Han Solo's soul.

In the old version, Solo shot first in his cantina showdown with a bounty hunter. But in the new one, Lucas addressed this moral dilemma with a slick edit that showed Greedo firing first. Thus, Solo was not a murderer but a mere scoundrel on the way to redemption.

"Lucas wanted to make sure that people knew that Han didn't shoot someone in cold blood," said broadcaster Dick Staub. "That would raise serious questions about his character, because we all know that murder is absolutely wrong."

The "Star Wars" films do, at times, have a strong sense of good and evil.

Yet in the climactic scene of the new "Revenge of the Sith," the evil Darth Vader warns his former master: "If you're not with me, you're my enemy." Obi-Wan Kenobi replies, "Only a Sith deals in absolutes."

Say what? If that is true, how did Lucas decide it was wrong for Solo to gun down a bounty hunter? Isn't that a moral absolute? If so, why are absolutes absolutely wrong in the saga's latest film? Good questions, according to Staub.

While we're at it, the Jedi knights keep saying they must resist the "dark side" of the mysterious, deistic Force. But they also yearn for a "chosen one" who will "bring balance" to the Force, a balance between good and evil.

"There is this amazing internal inconsistency in Lucas that shows how much conflict there is between the Eastern religious beliefs that he wants to embrace and all those Judeo-Christian beliefs that he grew up with," said Staub, author of a book for young people entitled "Christian Wisdom of the Jedi Masters."

"I mean, you're supposed to balance the light and the dark? How does that work?"

The key is that Lucas, who calls himself a "Buddhist Methodist," believes all kinds of things, even when the beliefs clash. This approach allows the digital visionary to take chunks of the world's major religions and swirl them in the blender of his imagination. Thus, the Force contains elements of Judaism, Christianity, animism, Hinduism, Buddhism, Taoism and even Islam.

None of this is surprising. Lucas merely echoes the beliefs of many artists in his generation and those who have followed. But the czar of "Star Wars" also has helped shape the imaginations of millions of spiritual consumers. His fun, nonjudgmental faith was a big hit at the mall.

It is impossible, said Staub, to calculate the cultural impact of this franchise since the 1977 release of the first film — "Star Wars: Episode IV, A New Hope." The films have influenced almost all moviegoers, but especially Americans 40 and under.

"I don't think there is anything coherent that you could call the Gospel According to Star Wars," stressed Staub. "But I do think there are things we can learn from Star Wars. . . . I think what we have here is a teachable moment, a point at which millions of people are talking about what it means to choose the dark side or the light side.

"Who wants the dark side to win? Most Americans want to see good triumph over evil, but they have no solid reasons for why they do. They have no idea what any of this has to do with their lives."

Staub is especially concerned about young "Star Wars" fans. He believes that many yearn for some kind of mystical religious experience, taught by masters who hand down ancient traditions and parables that lead to truths that have stood the test of time, age after age. These young people "want to find their Yoda, but they don't think real Yodas exist anymore," especially not in the world of organized religion, he said.

In the end, it's easier to go to the movies.

Meanwhile, many traditional religious leaders bemoan the fact that they cannot reach the young. So they try to modernize the faith instead of digging back to ancient mysteries and disciplines, said Staub.

"So many churches are choosing to go shallow, when many young people want to go deep," he said. "There are people who just want to be entertained. But there are others who want to be Jedis, for real."

POP MEDIA, REAL LIFE

If there is anything that we Americans agree on, it is that advertisements have little or no effect on us.

We say that we tune out the radio ads. We flip past those pages — OK, most of them — in our favorite magazines. We hope to buy one of those digital boxes that zap the television commercials altogether. You know the drill.

Meanwhile, ads rain down minute by minute, year after year. We like to talk about the impact on the young, citing studies that claim that by high school the typical American has seen a million or so ads on television. We sigh. If we were honest, we would then remember that most of us — baby boomers and younger — grew up after the mass-media Big Boom, and we were once young.

The commercials are the perfect symbol of the mass media and its role in our lives, a steady drizzle of images, information and emotions that help shape who we are. The ads provide the funds that fuel the media. If the ads do not work to one degree or another, then the system shuts down.

Just ask Father John F. Kavanaugh.

Kavanaugh is a Jesuit who leads the ethics program at St. Louis

University. But he is better known as the Catholic progressive who wrote the famous book "Following Christ in a Consumer Society." For years, Kavanaugh has lectured and written about materialism, in the commercial sense of that word, and his work is full of haunting phrases, like this quote from the late Pope John Paul II: "We are in danger of being owned by the things that we own."

In the late 1980s and early 1990s, the Jesuit followed pop culture down to its deepest roots and began studying the "spirituality of advertising." You may want to read that last phrase again. It's a bit scary if you think about it.

Once, during a lecture to some Catholic-school seventh graders, Kavanaugh asked the students to name as many world leaders as they could. The class came up with only 12, starting with the pope and the president. On a hunch, the priest asked them to name brands of designer jeans. The class quickly assembled a list of 50 or more. How about brands of beer? That list hit 40. Many of the students could sing the relevant jingles.

It didn't take long for Kavanaugh to realize what he was dealing with, as he collected samples of the ads. Put it all together, and what you have is a "video catechism" of what it means to be alive. It is especially telling how early in life ads begin targeting the young with erotic images and sexualizing their desires and their appearance. Many of these ads seem intentionally depressing, as if the creators realize that sad young people purchase more goods than those who are happy.

Other advertisements were tapping into even deeper desires, ranging from whiffs of Eternity perfume to Calvin Klein diaper covers to Mercedes-Benz automobiles dying and being reincarnated as newer models. "Seventeen" magazine once had an advertisement featuring a young girl holding a new issue with the caption: "Her Bible." Then there was the image of a roomful of people, each watching her or his own television under the headline "Peace on Earth."

"This is not just a psychological system," Kavanaugh once told a

Denver audience. "It is a theological system. . . . This is our culture's ultimate system of values."[1]

Truth is, visual advertisements are merely the first step in a kind of mass-media sacramental system. Here is how I like to state it:

Step 1: See this image, experience this feeling, feel this need.

Step 2: Buy and consume this product.

Step 3: Accept, by faith, that using or consuming the product will help you become the person in the image. The goal is to be able to say, "I am the kind of person who consumes this product."

This is a sacramental system. Whether they realize it or not, millions of people are making professions of faith at the shopping mall, taking Communion with their charge cards. This transcends logic. Media theorists Luigi and Alessandra MacLean Manca once noted that consumers tend to act toward a product as if it had a soul or a personality. "The function of advertising is therefore to suggest or even create this soul in the minds of the consumers," they wrote. "This is obviously a pseudo-spirituality. . . . It seems likely that we actually have a great spiritual void."[2]

This is our culture. It affects how we live and work. It helps shape how we raise our children and spend our paychecks. It even affects how we worship. And all the people said, "Amen."

LOOKING FOR A NEW GOD, A FRESH CREED?

February 2001

When it comes to answering life's big questions, the World Wide Web offers more research options than you can wiggle a mouse at.

Trying to find the right used car? Doing homework to find an appropriate college for your firstborn child? Are you a cat person or a dog person? What breed?

Perhaps you wake up in the middle of the night wondering if you need a new god or a fresh creed. Are you a liberal Protestant kind of person or a Hindu person, a Baptist or a Scientologist, a Reform Jew or a neopagan?

Want to find out? Then go to www.SelectSmart.com/Religion and click your way through Curt and Lorie Anderson's new and improved "Belief System Selector" site that covers two dozen world religions. Then you can tell them how happy or furious you are about the results. But don't ask about their religious ties. You can ask, but they won't tell.

"People have accused us of being part of every imaginable religious group in the world," said Curt Anderson. "A lot of people accuse us of being members of their religion, only they think that we've totally messed it up. Or they feel really threatened and they think that what we believe must be the total opposite of what they believe."

Lorie Anderson interjected: "Some people say, 'You must be Scientologists.' Other people think we're a Buddhist front. . . . A lot of people think we're Unitarians. It seems that if you go through and click on answers randomly, the test almost always tells you that you're a Unitarian Universalist. Of course, maybe that says something about Unitarians."

Cue the rim shot. One patron even claimed to have received a mixed test score of "100 percent Unitarian-Universalist" and "100 percent Jehovah's Witness." Sure enough, the writer e-mailed them the old joke: "You know what you get when you cross a Jehovah's Witness with a Unitarian? Someone who knocks on doors for no apparent reason."

The Andersons created SelectSmart.com three years ago, combining her social work and psychology skills with his experience in marketing and advertising. Their Ashland, Ore., home base is near the California border, which means they live in one of America's most complex regions when it comes to religion and, of course, technology.

So far, they have written or endorsed 200 "selector" programs to help people make choices affecting everything from hobbies to careers, from vacation spots to romance. The site includes links to nearly 2,000 other tests written by volunteers. At the peak of the campaign season, their presidential-candidate selector was receiving 80,000 visitors a day.

Since making its debut last August, the religion selector has been attracting 7,000 users a day, and the site now includes advanced quizzes to help fundamentalists, Jews, Gnostics, agnostics, pagans, Muslims and others further refine their options. The site includes scores of links to official Web sites representing the various churches, movements and traditions.

Lorie Anderson said she worked on the religion quiz off and on for at least six months and has continued to fine-tune her text, based on user feedback. The goal was to find issues that united the faiths — creation, evil, salvation, suffering — in order to provide some structure. Then she had to pinpoint doctrinal differences in order to sift through the users and pin on some theological labels.

The results often yield strange bedfellows. Orthodox Jews, for example, have more in common with Muslims than with Reform Jews. Liberal Protestants have more in common with pagans than with evangelical Protestants. Liberal Quakers resemble Hindus, while orthodox Quakers may hang out with the Mormons.

The test still isn't perfect. In particular, the Andersons have struggled to break the Christian doctrine of the Trinity down into bytes of computer data. Is God a "corporeal spirit (has a body)" or an "incorporeal spirit"?

"That's a tough one," said Curt Anderson. "Christians believe that Jesus had a body, yet God the Father does not. Yet they're both in the Trinity. . . . We're still working on that one."

"Right," said his wife. "Words mean a whole lot when you start trying to describe who or what God is or isn't. . . . When it comes to words, religious people get really picky."

FAITH POPCORN'S SPIRITUAL COCKTAILS

May 2000

Way back in the 1990s, Faith Popcorn had a sports car with a driver's seat that could be programmed to fit three different people, making each feel comfortable with a simple click.

This perfectly symbolized what the hip market analyst calls "Egonomics," which is what happens when Information Age consumers feel swamped and depersonalized and demand products that let them wallow in "me, myself and I."

"We Americans are the most self-analyzed and self-important people on the planet," argued Popcorn, in "Clicking," the bestseller that summarizes her work. "We know ourselves and we want to define ourselves — not to be told how to live and what to buy. We demand choices."

But at the same time, her BrainReserve company is convinced consumers want spiritual roots. This is a trend she calls "anchoring." So what happens when "Egonomics" collides with "anchoring" — pews that adjust to fit the individual worshipper? You got it.

"The future will be so radically different from anything we've known before, that having a spiritual connection will become more profoundly important," claims Popcorn, answering questions on her

Web site. "Spirituality and religion, however, will become much more self-defined. In essence, people will mix and pour their own religious cocktails.

"There will be a morphing of traditional religious practices and denominations. . . . We'll see some people at the center of organized religions react to this by becoming more and more fundamentalist."

Popcorn has always used sweeping, almost messianic language — pushing TrendBank themes such as "icon toppling," "S.O.S. (Save Our Society)," with its call for "moral transformation through marketing," and her modern believers are now seeking meaning by "clanning" in informal "mystical tribes" that unite around shared joys or pains.

This kind of talk comes easy for a Jewish girl who spent part of her childhood in Catholic schools in Shanghai, with a father who was a lawyer who worked for what became the U.S. Central Intelligence Agency.

As a young woman, the future futurist dreamed of a career in New York's theaters but ended up as an ad copywriter. One mentor couldn't pronounce her name — Faith Plotkin — and christened her Faith Popcorn. In 1974, she helped start BrainReserve and, in 1991, wrote "The Popcorn Report." The rest is the opposite of history.

In the upcoming book "EVEolution," Popcorn and co-writer Lys Marigold dissect the role women are playing in the marketplace and culture. The key is that Americans, led by female consumers, don't shop for a particular brand of product just to buy it. Instead, they want to "join a brand" and make it a source of identity. This is even true in religion.

In other words, Americans are not just shopping on the Internet, at the mall or in mass media. They are defining who they are and who they are not. This is political, this is spiritual and this process becomes especially important when consumers believe their lives are not "clicking."

For Popcorn, the essence of our age is contained in that word, *click*, which she describes with born-again fervor. People have to let go and take little leaps of faith — including at home and work. When enough people begin to leap in the same direction, the result is a cultural trend, one solid enough to last for a decade or longer.

To the individual consumer, this feels highly personal.

"Too many of us spend our lives feeling slightly off-kilter, slightly out of step and out of synch with our expectations," notes Popcorn. "Something isn't clicking: a job, an idea, a product, a place, the sum total of what we're doing and where we're going. We fumble around trying to find the right combination to break into a new life."

Then something clicks, and people find "control, focus, clarity, success." This is not a merely secular process.

"We're all at the start of a great awakening, a time of spiritual and religious revival," insists Popcorn. "What's different about this awaking is that there's very little agreement on who or what God is, what constitutes worship and what this outpouring means. . . . The need to Anchor has found expression in all of the world's religions, whether they celebrate the Old and New Testament God, Buddha, Allah, Brahma, unnamed higher powers or self-discovery."

A BRAND NAME FOR YOUR SOUL

April 2001

Anyone strolling through the National Funeral Directors Association convention could catch glimpses of baby boomer heaven.

The Baltimore exhibits included "fairway to heaven" caskets for those especially devout golfers and NASCAR models for true fans who have seen their last race, at least in this life. The goal, said a convention spokesman, is to offer dying consumers the same kinds of choices that they demanded in life.

What's next? Allowing people to defray some funeral expenses via product-endorsement logos, like the ones on golf caps and racing cars? If there is a Harley-Davidson casket — yes, there is one — can a Lexus model be far behind? Could a user reboot his Microsoft casket?

I cannot answer such soul-wrenching questions. But every year I do mark this column's anniversary by weaving together a few bizarre items that loiter in my files. For year No. 13, the designer-casket news snapped into place next to a story from The Financial Times.

It seems that the prestigious Young & Rubicam advertising agency is convinced many brand names have become substitute religions. They provide meaning for millions of believers who gradually become what they consume while taking Communion, so to speak, at the mall.

"The brands that are succeeding are those with strong beliefs and original ideas," said an agency report. "They are also the ones that have the passion and energy to change the world, and to convert people to their way of thinking though outstanding communications."

When true believers think of Apple, Calvin Klein, Gatorade, Volvo, MTV, Starbucks, Nike and Virgin, they don't just think of products. These uncompromising "belief brands" help establish a sense of identity, according to Young & Rubicam. They are icons that define lives.

Are advertisers our new priests and evangelists? With that in mind, ponder this.

- Up in Vancouver, some Canadian Christians were not amused by "Second Coming" ads for the Playland Amusement Park, which included a turnstile clicking ominously to "666." The park had just added two new rides — the "Hellevator" and the "Revelation."

- While many were offended by "Yo' Mama's Last Supper," a work of modern art that depicted Jesus as a nude black woman, an exhibit in Chicago offered up "The Last Pancake Breakfast," with Christ as Mrs. Butterworth.

- Leaders of Southern California's 600,000 Muslims were not amused by Los Angeles Times ads juxtaposing images of bikini-clad California women with women in Islamic attire, linked by the slogan "Connecting Us to The Times." The newsroom staff protested, too, and the ads were soon phased out.

- In other multicultural news, shoppers noted changes in Nativity images last year in London. In a few, Joseph had been omitted to avoid offending female single parents. Wire-service reports also described tableaus in which a female figure replaced Joseph, to appeal to what the survey called those with "Sapphic," or lesbian, "inclinations."

- Here's another British innovation with mass appeal. The Anglican vicar of All Saints Parish in Guildford advertised a "Harry Potter" service complete with wizards, costumes, broomsticks, "Muggle songs" (hymns) and a nonflying version of a "quidditch" game. The church's doorway was decorated as the King's Cross Station platform on which J.K. Rowling's characters catch the train to the Hogwarts School of Witchcraft and Wizardry. There was even a serpent banner for the ominous House of Slytherin, along with other Hogwarts decorations. The London Times said other parishes quickly requested copies of the liturgy.

- Can one purchase inner peace and salvation? The satirists at www.TheOnion.com have their doubts. They published a fake press release for an imaginary snack meant to ease the "hideously bleak emptiness of modern life. . . . We're proud to introduce T.C. McCrispee's as the antidote you've been reaching out for. Our tasty new snack cracker will, if only for a few lovely moments, significantly lessen the aching, gnawing angst that haunts your very soul."

Participants in taste tests testified that the "satisfying crunch distracted them from the parade of tears that is life." A faux spokesperson summed up the campaign: "We're selling more than a cracker here. We're selling the salty, unctuous illusion of happiness."

BOBOS "R" US

January 2001

Every Saturday, journalist David Brooks and his family can choose between three services at their synagogue in Washington, D.C.

Rabbis lead a mainstream, almost Protestant, rite in the sanctuary. Then there is an informal Havurah (fellowship) service led by laypeople, including a 45-minute talk-back session. The erudite leaders often pause to explain why the Torah's more judgmental and dogmatic passages don't mean what they seem to mean.

Finally, throngs of young adults pack the wonderfully named Traditional Egalitarian service, which features longer Torah readings, a rigorous approach to liturgy and what Brooks called a "somewhat therapeutic" seminar blending spirituality and daily life.

"It can get pretty New Age-y," said Brooks at his Weekly Standard office. "It's as if you're in an Orthodox shul and then Oprah Winfrey comes on."

It was a rabbi in Montana who gave Brooks the perfect word — *Flexidoxy* — to describe this faith. This is what happens when Americans try to baptize their souls in freedom and tradition, radical individualism and orthodoxy, all at the same time. One scholar found a Methodist pastor's daughter who calls herself a "Methodist Taoist Native American Quaker Russian Orthodox Buddhist Jew."

It doesn't make any sense, but it looks good and feels right. And that's the key to the hearts of the intellectuals, artists, politicians and entrepreneurs who came to power after the 1960s. When it comes to the culture wars, they are lovers, not fighters.

Brooks calls them "Bobos," which is shorthand for "bourgeois bohemians." Their yin-yang worldview — part '60s idealism, part '80s work ethic — now dominates academia and politics, Hollywood and, recently, Wall Street. But the Bobos, said Brooks, struggle when they try to fly solo through life's major transition times, such as marriage, birth and death.

"Can you have freedom as well as roots? Can you still worship God even if you take it upon yourself to decide that many of the Bible's teachings are wrong?" he asks in his rollicking book "Bobos in Paradise."

"Can you establish ritual and order in your life if you are driven by an inner imperative to experiment constantly with new things? . . . The Bobos are trying to build a house of obligation on a foundation of choice."

The book's spirituality chapter ends with a glimpse of "Bobo Heaven," in which a sophisticated Angel of Death leaves a materialistic superwoman to spend eternity in her perfect Montana summer house, with National Public Radio on every channel. Is this heaven or hell?

Brooks stressed that millions of Americans are sincerely struggling to live better lives, while simultaneously refusing to accept traditional religious creeds and dogmas. They have been taught, after all, that they must call their own shots, write their own creeds. He quips, "You've got to think outside the box. . . . You've got to be on the edge. You've got to be outside the box that's on the edge."

For Bobos and their followers, said Brooks, the idea of "one, universal truth is not even something that they have consciously rejected. This concept is not a part of their world. They have never even really considered the idea that one religion might be true and all the others false, or even that there is one true way to approach the moral universe, and all the others are false."

But Bobos do not consider themselves moral relativists. They do make judgments. They even have creeds, said Brooks, but they are built on concerns about aesthetics, health, safety, science, self-esteem and, especially, achievement. This approach to life may even include an appreciation for "spirituality" and religious rituals. Bobos are willing to buy and consume many high-quality religious products and services.

"They have very concrete ways of faking a morality, especially when it comes to the rules that go with achievement," said Brooks. "You do whatever is best for your career and your long-term interests. . . . So when it comes to religion, they want to be very positive and upbeat. It's all about encouragement and grace. They avoid the bad parts, which means the judgmental parts."

The bottom line: Does your congregation have what it takes? Can it afford to be Bobo-friendly?

LENT: FASTING FROM TELEVISION
February 1999

Some people give up candy or soft drinks, while others sacrifice something as major as caffeine or meat.

So far, so good. However, Father Michael Buckley thinks most Roman Catholics, and members of other churches that observe

Lent, would find it easier to properly prepare to celebrate Easter if they took an even more drastic step — unplugging their televisions.

"The reality is that most people sacrifice small things at Lent in order to give the season a kind of a tone of self-sacrifice," said Father Buckley of Plainview, Neb., whose "On Media" column appears in about 90 Catholic newspapers. "People give up little things because we have trouble even thinking about making real sacrifices anymore. Seriously, most Catholics no longer see themselves as different from the culture around them. This really shows up at Lent."

Making a symbolic spiritual change isn't an end in itself, during the 40 days between Ash Wednesday and Easter, which this year is on April 4. In Eastern Orthodoxy, the season of Great Lent began with Forgiveness Sunday on Feb. 21 and ends with Pascha on April 11.

The goal is to create a zone of quiet for repentance and reflection. The defining signs of Lent are supposed to be fasting, prayer and alms giving, said Father Buckley. However, the season's message is usually drowned out by the noise of daily life. As radical as it sounds, one of the only ways to give Lent a fighting chance is to turn off, or to at least curtail the use of, the TVs scattered throughout most homes.

"You end up with more time for your family, for prayer, for the church, for life in general," he said. "But I think most people would find it much harder to give up television during Lent than to give up meat."

It's hard to fight this kind of battle without practical strategies.

For some people, a good starting point would be spending two or more hours reading for each hour that they watch television, said evangelical media critic Doug LeBlanc, in a recent Moody magazine column. Then, when he does turn on the TV, he has vowed to hit the mute button during every commercial.

"Commercials are not only loud and intrusive," noted LeBlanc, "but they sell a particularly noxious snake oil known as commercialism. I have enough trouble resisting the siren call of narcissism without reinforcing it during every commercial break."

But the big problem is that people use mass media — especially television news, sports, talk radio and music — as pseudo-shopping-mall "white noise" to cover gaps in their lives that hint at loneliness or a need for self-reflection, said LeBlanc. Clearly, many fear silence.

It's also possible to make better decisions about what to watch, as well as how much to watch, said James Breig, a columnist in Credo, an alternative Catholic weekly in Ann Arbor, Mich. Some could begin by listing their five favorite shows and then swearing off one of them, to invest that time in spiritual books. High-quality religious programs also turn up occasionally on history and arts channels, and some parishes have begun collecting libraries of videotapes.

And it might help to put a Bible or prayer book near the TV Guide or the remote control.

"In an average week," Breig asked his readers, "which do you do more often: watch TV or pray? Think of how often you say, 'There's nothing on,' and then watch that nothing."

The overarching problem is that, all too often, church leaders and members choose to ignore the role that all those televisions play in most homes and in the culture at large. Mass media are, in fact, the channels through which most people receive the stories, images and values that shape their lives — hour after hour, day by day, season after season.

"The THING called a television, the actual box with a screen on it and some speakers, can do some good," said Father Buckley. "The problem is how people let television and the media take over their lives. That's a spiritual issue. I don't think that it's a reach to say that the role television plays in most modern homes is evil."

CATHOLIC COLLEGE CULTURE WARS

August 2003

Anyone trying to understand the Catholic college culture wars can start with the commencement address by Cardinal Francis Arinze at Georgetown University.

Media coverage was guaranteed, since many listed the Nigerian prelate as a top contender to succeed Pope John Paul II. Who knew he would dare to mention sex and marriage?

"The family is under siege," said Arinze. "It is opposed by an anti-life mentality as seen in contraception, abortion, infanticide and euthanasia. It is scorned and banalized by pornography, desecrated by fornication and adultery, mocked by homosexuality, sabotaged by irregular unions and cut in two by divorce."

A theology professor walked out, as did some outraged students. Seventy faculty members signed a letter of protest. But traditional Catholics began asking a burning question: Why was it shocking for a cardinal to defend Catholic doctrines on a Catholic campus?

These fires are still smoldering as students return to America's 223 Catholic colleges and universities. The Arinze controversy also reinforced some controversial statistics suggesting that four years on most Catholic campuses may actually harm young Catholic souls.

"What we are seeing is a battle between orthodox Christian beliefs and the moral relativism that is becoming more powerful in many religious groups," said Patrick Reilly, president of the Cardinal Newman Society, a fiercely pro-Vatican educational network.

"Catholic, Protestant, Jewish, you name it. This battle is going on in all denominations and, of course, in their schools."

Reilly bulldogs Catholic trends. Thus, the Newman network and the conservative Catholic World Report paid University of California at Los Angeles researchers to isolate Catholic data in their 2001 Higher Education Research Institute survey. The new report focused on students who were freshmen in 1997 and seniors in 2001, documenting changes in beliefs and behavior.

The big question: Was the faith commitment shown in fundraising and recruiting materials reflected in the day-to-day reality in dorms and classrooms?

These data covered only 38 campuses and emphasized some of American Catholicism's most influential, progressive institutions, such as Notre Dame, Creighton, Gonzaga, St. John's, Loyola Marymount and Xavier. The results sparked fierce debate, especially about issues of sexuality and Catholic doctrine.

The survey found that 37.9 percent of Catholic freshmen at Catholic colleges said abortion should be legal, while as seniors, 51.7 percent said that. Also, 27.5 percent of Catholic freshmen believed premarital sex was acceptable for people who "really like each other." As seniors, 48 percent took that view. As freshmen, 52.4 percent favored legal marriages for homosexuals. As seniors, 69.5 percent held this view.

As freshmen, two-thirds of the Catholic students said they frequently attended Mass and one-third did so occasionally. As seniors, 13 percent had stopped attending and nearly half attended occasionally. Nine percent left the church altogether.

"You would think that going to Catholic colleges such as these would strengthen your faith," said Reilly. "That does not appear to be the case."

The powers that be in Catholic higher education were infuriated, saying the report twisted the UCLA statistics and consistently chose the worst possible interpretations. Clearly, the Cardinal Newman Society was striving to create as much tension as possible between the Vatican and mainstream Catholic schools.

"You may have launched a process that is now out of control," said

Monika Hellwig, president of the Association of Catholic Colleges and Universities, in a letter to Reilly and copied to 11 bishops. "We ask you in a spirit of Catholic charity to stop attacking Catholic institutions, and most of all to be sure that you and your network of student informers not publish anything that is not demonstrably true, properly in context and balanced in presentation."

This data was very limited, agreed Reilly. The way to move forward would be for these two groups to work together on an in-depth survey, visiting a larger sample of campuses — including openly conservative Catholic colleges and universities. But such a project would be difficult, said Reilly, due to clashing goals and worldviews.

"We know that what we are seeking is countercultural," he said. "Of course, what this pope is advocating is obviously counter-cultural. What we want to see is not normal. At least, it's not what people on the street or even many people in your typical Catholic parish would call normal."

PRAYING WITH
THE DIGITAL NATIVES
February 2001

It's hard to move into a new office without spending some time exploring the past.

Digging into a 20-year-old box, Drew University evangelism professor Leonard Sweet time-warped back to his doctoral studies as he dug through layers of onionskin paper smudged with real ink and an ancient substance called Wite-Out.

"I went from being an archeologist to, as I dug deeper, a paleontologist. I found carbon paper. This thing needed to be carbon-dated, it was so old," he said, speaking at a global forum for leaders from 150 Christian campuses. "I looked at this and I said, 'Sweet! This is from a defunct civilization.' But you know what? It was from MY civilization. I'm a Gutenberg person. . . . My world was shaped by the book."

Now that world has passed away, even if the rulers of many fortresses haven't noticed.

Sweet believes there is one fact of life that clergy and religious educators must learn — pronto. If they refuse to do so, he said, they will have as much success as someone who tries to make "a credit-card call from a rotary telephone." Here is that fact: "If you are born before 1962, you are an immigrant. If you are born after 1962, you are a native."

Calendar age isn't everything, Sweet conceded. It's theoretically possible to be a 70-year-old native or a 20-year-old immigrant, in the land of digital dialogues and postmodern parables. But immigrants who want to leap from the old "Carpe Diem" world into what he called the culture of "Carpe Manana" must be open to learning languages, customs and skills from the natives.

"I am an immigrant," he said. "I am having Ellis Island experiences every day."

While trained in church history, Sweet is best known for his attempts to peer into the future. He draws rave reviews as a speaker in both mainline and evangelical gatherings, while writing waves of books with trendy titles such as "Quantum Spirituality" and his futuristic trilogy "SoulSalsa," "AquaChurch" and "SoulTsunami."

The history of education has included three landmark events, said Sweet, speaking in Orlando to leaders of the Council for Christian Colleges and Universities. These were the creation of the Greek alphabet, the invention of the printing press and the arrival of the World Wide Web. Colleges and seminaries can handle the first two, but most are doing little to face the implications of that third shift, other than buying hardware and software. They have rewired their campuses, but not their brains.

Immigrants lead these institutions and many have replaced their rose-tinted glasses with "black-out shades," said Sweet. Nevertheless, they know the natives are restless.

When seeking answers to big questions, the natives don't want to sit in orderly rows and sing tiny sets of hymn verses interspersed with bulletin-board announcements, all of which precede a long lecture called a sermon. When they sing, they prefer flowing songs that seem to last forever while they stand enraptured in an atmosphere of worship.

They are not pew people. What they want, said Sweet, is faith, and even education, that is "experiential," "participatory," "image-based" and "connective." They want a faith that is timeless and timely, at the same time. They want truth that touches all of their senses.

This will be traumatic for leaders of America's aging mainstream religious groups, said Sweet. They feel comfortable with people with blue hair, "unless it shows up on a 16-year-old kid." Many worship in sanctuaries containing images of a Savior with pierced hands and feet, yet they panic when young people show up who "look like they fell out of a tackle box."

Truth is, these natives are swimming in information, but they lack perspective, he said. They don't need the help or permission of authority figures to find their own information about politics, technology, morality and even religion.

That is when the immigrants must be willing to listen carefully to their questions, said Sweet. The natives have information, but many are asking, "Now, what do I do with it? How do I test what is good and what is bad information? How do I turn that information into knowledge and then that knowledge into wisdom?"

JUST ANOTHER SUNDAY AT SADDLEBACK

March 2000

LAKE FOREST, Calif. — The Saddleback Community Church bleachers were still filling up when the jazzy Latino pre-service music faded and, with a "One, two, three!" countdown, the 13-piece band rocked into their opening hymn.

"I wanna be like you. Live every day, the way that you want me to," sang the throng, watching the JumboTrons. "It's getting better. I read your letter. These are the words you said to me. Love the Lord with all your heart. Love your neighbor as yourself. These are the things that you must do, and my grace will see you through. . . . It's all about love. Hey!"

Saddleback looks like a textbook megachurch, the kind that keeps inspiring sociologists to rush to their computers. The Rev. Rick Warren and friends mailed 15,000 invitations to their first service in 1980, and the church had 10,000 members before it built a sanctuary. Today, 15,000 or more attend five "seeker-friendly" weekend services. The sunny baptismal pool welcomes a river of newcomers, with 1,638 baptized in 1999.

Outside the 3,000-seat worship center, booths offered programs for families, blended families, single parents, separated men, separated women and people struggling with almost every difficulty life can offer. Inside, the choir bounced through a reggae chorus, an oldie from 1979 and a gospel-rock anthem. Then Warren took center stage, dressed down in khakis and a black knit shirt.

"We've been looking at thinking clearly about your problems, about your relationships, about change, about sex, about stress," he said, starting one of many strolls away from the traditional pulpit.

"But there's one area where people are more confused than probably any other area. It causes more divorces than sex. And it is finances; it's 'Till debt do us part.'"

The crowd laughed, because Warren is a witty storyteller and commentator on Orange County life. On this day, he told many in his flock: "You're spending money you don't have on things that you don't need to impress people you don't even like." This creates Saddleback Valley syndrome, with dreams and debts creating workaholism, then exhaustion, then depression, then shopping sprees, then more debt.

But this wasn't a megachurch sermonette for folks used to clutching a TV remote. Warren regularly preaches between 50 minutes and an hour, working his way through a dozen Scripture passages and waves of illustrations from the news and daily life. Seeker-friendly sermons do not have to be short and shallow, he said.

"The idea that postmodern people will not listen to a 'talking head' for 45 minutes is pure myth," he said. "Of course, most people, including many preachers, couldn't hold an audience for 10 minutes. But that's due to their communication style, not the supposed short attention span of unbelievers. Any communicator who is personal, passionate, authentic and applies the Scriptures to real life will have no trouble holding the attention of our generation."

Critics may scoff, but this Southern Baptist congregation is committed to developing techniques to help churches with 150 members, as well as 15,000. Saddleback services rarely include comedy and drama, because small churches struggle to find talented writers and actors. Saddleback rarely uses high-tech media in its services, because small churches don't have the resources to do so.

That's OK. Warren said that "if all seekers were looking for was a quality production, they'd stay home and watch TV, where millions are spent to produce half-hour programs."

But most of Warren's sermons do include breaks in which church members offer testimonies — sometimes chatty, sometimes wrenching — about how their lives have been changed by prayer, Bible study, giving and service. Why do this? Because all churches can ask members to offer testimonies.

Churches don't have to be shallow to appeal to the heads and hearts of unbelievers, stressed Warren. In fact, just the opposite is true.

"Unbelievers wrestle with the same deep questions believers have," he said. "Who am I? Where did I come from? Where am I going? Does life make sense? Why is there suffering and evil in the world? What is my purpose in life? How can I learn to get along with people? These are certainly not shallow issues."

MYSTERIOUS ECHOES OF GUNSHOTS
September 1999

It's hard to read any of the sermons that the Rev. Martin Luther King Jr. preached about death and heaven without hearing echoes of gunshots.

"The minute you conquer the fear of death, at that moment you are free," he said in 1963. "I submit to you that if a man hasn't discovered something that he will die for, he isn't fit to live."

Decades later, these words still inspire faith and courage, said social activist Johann Christoph Arnold, who marched with King in the civil rights movement. That's why the patriarch of the nine Bruderhof communes in the U.S., England and Australia included this quotation in his most recent book, "Seeking Peace."

This was the book that Cassie Bernall and other teenagers at West Bowles Community Church were supposed to have discussed on the evening of April 20. After that tragic day at Columbine High

School, Bernall's parents showed Arnold her copy of "Seeking Peace," with its handwritten notes for the study session that was never held.

Cassie had boldly underlined King's thoughts on death. Did she hear echoes of gunshots?

"Why did those words speak to her at such a young age? It is such a great mystery," said Arnold. "But I do know this. She had found something she was willing to live for, and even to die for, and that made all the difference in her life."

Here is what Cassie wrote in a 1998 note her parents discovered after her death: "I try to stand up for my faith at school. I will die for my God. I will die for my faith. It's the least I can do for Christ dying for me."

Cassie Bernall was one of the Columbine students who was asked, at gunpoint, "Do you believe in God?" Her story has been spread by news reports and chains of Internet sites hailing her as a martyr in the true sense of that ancient title in Christendom.

Now her mother has written her own tribute, entitled "She Said Yes." Because of the ties between Cassie, her church and Arnold's writings, Misty Bernall's 140-page memoir has been published by the Plough Publishing House, which is linked to the tiny Bruderhof movement, with its commitment to pacifism, simple living and the sanctity of life.

In the wake of Littleton, many Americans — politicians, preachers and pundits — keep arguing about the "larger issues" that supposedly led to the bloodshed, notes Misty Bernall. She is convinced parents must focus on more personal issues closer to home.

"Why, when parents and lawmakers are calling for gun control and an end to TV violence, are our young crying out for relationships?" she asks. "Why, when we offer them psychologists and counselors and experts on conflict resolution, are they going to youth groups and looking for friends? Why, when everyone else is apportioning blame and constructing new defenses, are they talking about a change of the heart?"

Nevertheless, "She Said Yes" makes it clear that Cassie's parents repeatedly had to say no, as they pulled her away from peers involved in the occult. Her mother reprints passages from letters in which Cassie and a friend pondered suicide and murder. The Bernalls taped telephone calls, searched their daughter's room, took evidence to the police and, finally, moved to another neighborhood. Cassie raged against it all, until her life was changed during a church youth retreat.

Brad and Misty Bernall refused to give up, noted Arnold, and made radical changes in their own lives, as well as in the life of their daughter. All of this took time, energy and sacrifice. Cassie's new life was rooted in weekly patterns of fellowship, prayer, reading and service projects with her family and new friends. They ate pizza and went skiing, but also helped leukemia patients and built homes for the poor. Cassie traded vampires and "death rock" for poetry and photography.

"Cassie would never have said yes in that final moment, unless she had said yes so many other times before that," said Arnold. "She had to say yes to many wonderful experiences in her new life, before she had the strength to say the ultimate yes when that moment came. We must not forget that."

INTOLERANT CHRISTIANS IN THE PUBLIC SQUARE

January 2000

As they lurched through a blinding snowstorm over Tokyo, the Rev. Billy Graham watched as the nervous pilot focused single-mindedly on his cockpit instruments.

When it came time to land that plane, the pilot and the air-traffic controllers followed a dogmatic set of rules. They were intolerant of errors, and Graham was thankful for that.

"I did not want these men to be broad-minded," he said in a sermon that is currently circulating on the Internet. "I knew that our lives depended on it."

There are times, said the evangelist, when tolerance is bad. For centuries, Christians have proclaimed that the journey from earth to heaven is like any other difficult journey. It is crucial to have accurate directions and a trustworthy pilot when souls are at stake. Thus, Jesus said, "I am the way and the truth and the life. No one comes to the Father except through me."

Jesus is intolerant, said Graham, when it comes to matters of salvation.

Try defending that stance on CNN. By the end of 1999, pundits and politicos were starting to suggest that evangelism equals hate speech.

The anonymous person who launched this text into cyberspace, with the title "Jesus Was Not Tolerant," has a good memory and a nose for news. The Billy Graham Evangelistic Association's records indicate that this sermon was delivered in 1956 before being published as an evangelistic tract in 1957, 1984 and 1996.

The bottom line: If the world's most famous evangelist preached the same sermon today, it would make headlines and draw flak on the evening news. It would be hard to imagine anyone making a more inflammatory statement than the one attributed to Jesus in the Gospel of John: "He who believes in the Son has everlasting life; and he who does not believe the Son shall not see life, but the wrath of God abides on him."

Questions about heaven, hell and salvation have been lurking between the lines of many news stories. Politicians want to bless new ties binding the government and "faith-based charities," so long as workers don't proselytize. GOP frontrunner George W. Bush said Jesus saved his soul and that other people may not understand what that means. Evangelical military chaplains have said they are being told to preach safe, nonjudgmental sermons — or else.

While visiting India, Pope John Paul II said "there can be no true evangelization without the explicit proclamation of Jesus as Lord." The heir to Graham's pulpit — his son Franklin — angered many non-evangelicals when he urged non-Christians at the Columbine High School memorial service to turn to Jesus before it was too late. The list goes on and on.

Leaders of the 15.8 million-member Southern Baptist Convention have repeatedly refused to cease their efforts to evangelize all non-Christians, including Jews, Muslims and Hindus. The interfaith Council of Religious Leaders of Metropolitan Chicago cried foul and said an upcoming Southern Baptist evangelistic push "could contribute to a climate conducive to hate crimes" in the city.

Asked about President Clinton's view of this controversy, press secretary Joe Lockhart said the Southern Baptist in the White House is convinced that one of the new century's major challenges will be "dealing with intolerance and coming to grips with the long-held resentments between religions. So I think he's been very clear in his opposition to whatever organizations, including the Southern Baptists, that perpetuate ancient religious hatred."

Southern Baptist leaders immediately cried foul, accused Lockhart of being hateful and called for his resignation. The Rev. Morris Chapman, president of the SBC's executive committee, said: "It is the right of every person to agree or disagree with the internal doctrines of Christianity, but we believe for any governmental office to endeavor to pressure Christians to change their doctrines or practices is improper and reprehensible."

This conflict will not fade away.

There is no question that the First Amendment protects the free speech of non-Christians and others who are offended by intolerant, narrow-minded Christians who proclaim that Jesus is the only savior for all of humankind. Right now, the question appears to be whether Christian evangelists will retain their right to preach that message in the public square.

WORSHIP WARS IN THE PEWS
July 1999

The worshippers may gather in a candle-lit sanctuary and follow a liturgy of ancient texts and solemn chants, while gazing at Byzantine icons.

The singing, however, will be accompanied by waves of drums and electric guitars, and the result often sounds like a cross between Pearl Jam and the Monks of Santo Domingo de Silos. The icons, meanwhile, are digital images downloaded from the World Wide Web and projected on screens.

The people who are experimenting with these kinds of rites aren't interested in the bouncy baby boomer-friendly megachurch praise services that have dominated American Protestantism for a generation. They want to appeal to teens and young adults who consider "contemporary worship" shallow and old-fashioned and out of touch with their darker, more ironic take on life. They are looking for what comes next.

It might be smart to buy incense now, before prices rise.

"People are trying all kinds of things trying to find an edge," said the Rev. Daniel Harrell, a staff member of Boston's historic Park Street Church who is active in ministry to the so-called Generation X and other young adults.

"They'll go online and go to Brother Jim's icon page. Then they right-click with a mouse, save some icons and they're in business. The basic attitude is, 'It's old. It's real. Let's put it up on the screen and play a grinding grunge worship song. That'll be cool.'"

The result is what Harrell, writing in the journal Leadership, has called "post-contemporary worship." If previous generations of free-wheeling Protestants have tried to strip away layers of tradition and ritual in an attempt to appeal to modern people, some of today's emerging church planters are trying to add a few doses of beauty and mystery. They are trying to create — on their own terms — new traditions out of the pieces of old traditions.

It helps to realize that almost every church found in an American telephone book has been buffeted, for several decades, by changes caused by television, rock 'n' roll, the Internet and every other form of popular culture. Vatican II opened the door to neo-Protestant changes in Catholic hymnody and worship, while some influential Protestants have been digging into their ancient roots. Others have openly tried to incorporate elements of drama, humor and film into user-friendly services for the media age.

"While some churches are busy buying brand-new hymnals, others are discarding theirs, not to be replaced," noted John Witvliet, director of the Institute of Christian Worship at Calvin College. "Some churches are approaching such changes eagerly and expectantly; others are embroiled in 'worship wars.'"

If the baby boomers shunned churches that they thought were pompous and boring, then their pierced, tattooed and media-numbed children appear ready to shun churches that feel fake and frivolous. The key, according to Harrell, is that worship services must feel real. Services are judged to be authentic when they feel authentic.

"It's not that feeling has totally replaced doctrine or anything like that," he said. "The people who are doing this have doctrine. In fact, they are usually very, very conservative — almost fundamentalist.

But they may know little or nothing about the doctrines that actually go with the symbols and the rituals and the words they are using."

The final product is uneven, to say the least. Protestant piety collides with Catholic language, and Orthodox iconography is grafted into charismatic prayers. These experimental churches, noted Harrell, are almost always based on a "free church" concept of government in which all decisions are local. A shepherd and his flock can change from one style of worship to another with a show-of-hands vote in a midweek committee meeting, if they feel the need to do so.

"So people are borrowing things from all of these traditions, often without realizing that some of these symbols and rites may even clash with each other," he said. "It's easy to be cynical about this, but they really are searching for something. They are borrowing other people's images and rites and experiences, as part of their own search for something that feels authentic. They are trying to step into the experiences of others."

NOTES

Introduction

  1. ZZ Top lyrics, "Jesus Just Left Chicago."

  2. Barna, George and Hatch, Mark. *Boiling Point: Monitoring Cultural Shifts in the 21st Century.* (Ventura, CA. Regal, 2003), 188.

God and Popular Music

  1. "Bullet the Blue Sky," recorded by P.O.D.

  2. Gospel Music Association definition of gospel music.

  3. Van Halen lyrics, "Fire in the Hole."

Big Ideas on the Big Screen

  1. From an interview with the author.

  2. Haddon Robinson, 1990 sermon.

God on TV

  1. Meyers, Kenneth A. *All God's Children and Blue Suede Shoes: Christians and Popular Culture.* (Wheaton, IL, Crossway, 1989), 160.

  2. Briner, Robert. *Roaring Lambs.* (Grand Rapids, Zondervan, 2000), 28–29.

Pop Media, Real Life

  1. Father John F. Kavanaugh, from an interview with the author.

  2. Whetmore, Edward Jay. *Mediamerica, Mediaworld* (Wadsworth Publishing, 1993), 298.

INDEX

ABOUT THE AUTHOR

PROF. TERRY MATTINGLY writes the nationally syndicated "On Religion" column for the Scripps Howard News Service in Washington, D.C., and directs the Washington Journalism Center at the Council for Christian Colleges and Universities. He also leads the GetReligion.org website that critiques the mainstream media's coverage of religion news.

Mattingly's father was a pastor and his mother is a language arts teacher, so his interest in religion writing was no great surprise. He double-majored in journalism and history at Baylor University and then earned an M.A. at Baylor in Church-State Studies and an M.S. in communications at the University of Illinois in Urbana-Champaign.

Mattingly is a prodigal Texan who has never met a mountain he didn't love, as well as a music fanatic whose interests range from Celtic acoustic guitar to Russian chant. The Mattinglys are members of Holy Cross Orthodox Church in Linthicum, Md.